Alice's Adventures in Wonderland
and
Through the Looking-Glass

Nonsense, Sense, and Meaning

Twayne's Masterwork Series

Robert Lecker, General Editor

ALICE'S ADVENTURES IN WONDERLAND
and
THROUGH THE LOOKING-GLASS

Nonsense, Sense, and Meaning

Donald Rackin

Twayne Publishers • *New York*
Maxwell Macmillan Canada • *Toronto*
Maxwell Macmillan International • *New York   Oxford   Singapore   Sydney*

Twayne's Masterwork Studies No. 81

Alice's Adventures in Wonderland and *Through the Looking-Glass: Nonsense, Sense, and Meaning*

Donald Rackin

Twayne Publishers
Macmillan Publishing Company
866 Third Avenue
New York, New York 10022

Maxwell Macmillan Canada, Inc.
1200 Eglinton Avenue East
Suite 200
Don Mills, Ontario M3C 3N1

Macmillan Publishing Company is part of the Maxwell Communication Group of Companies.

Library of Congress Cataloging-in-Publication Data

Rackin, Donald.
    Alice's adventures in Wonderland and Through the looking glass : nonsense, sense, and meaning / Donald Rackin.
       p.   cm.—(Twayne's masterwork studies ; no. 81)
    Includes bibliographical references and index.
    ISBN 0-8057-9430-1.—ISBN 0-8057-8553-1 (pbk.)
    1. Carroll, Lewis, 1832–1898.   Alice's adventures in Wonderland.
    2. Carroll, Lewis, 1832–1898. Through the looking-glass.
    3. Children's stories, English—History and criticism.   4. Fantastic fiction, English—History and criticism.   I. Title. II. Series.
    PR4611.A73R34   1991
    823'.8—dc20
                                              91-20134

The paper used in this publication meets the minimum requirements of American National Standard for Information Sciences—Permanence of Paper for Printed Library Materials, ANSI Z39.48-1984. ∞™

10 9 8 7 6 5 4 3 2 1 (hc)
10 9 8 7 6 5 4 3 2 1 (pb)

Copyediting supervised by Barbara Sutton.
Book production by Janet Z. Reynolds.
Typeset by Huron Valley Graphics, Inc., Ann Arbor, Michigan

Printed in the United States of America.

To Phyllis and Ethel

Contents

Note on the References and Acknowledgments

For this study I have used the Norton Critical Edition of Lewis Carroll's masterworks, *Alice in Wonderland: Authoritative Texts of Alice's Adventures in Wonderland, Through the Looking-Glass, and The Hunting of the Snark: Backgrounds and Essays in Criticism,* ed. Donald J. Gray (New York: W. W. Norton, 1971). (A revised, second edition of this Norton Collection is scheduled for publication in 1992.) For clarity, the abbreviations *W* and *L* appear before the page citations.

In my Lewis Carroll studies over the past 30 years, I have been blessed with the invaluable encouragement and advice of many generous and learned friends, among them Nina Auerbach, Morton Cohen, Edward Guiliano, and James Kincaid. I am also grateful to the Lewis Carroll Society of North America and the Victorians Institute for the opportunity to present several papers that eventually grew into chapters of this book. But my greatest thanks go to my best advisor and dearest friend, Professor Phyllis Rackin of the University of Pennsylvania. Her astute readings, deep understanding, brilliant literary insights, and unerring editorial advice have helped me immeasurably. Without her this book would have never been written.

Chronology:
Lewis Carroll's Life and Works*

1832   Charles Lutwidge Dodgson (Lewis Carroll) born 27 January at the parsonage of Daresbury, a village in Cheshire. Charles is the third child and eldest son of the Reverend Charles Dodgson (later Archdeacon) and Frances Jane Lutwidge, first cousins married in 1827; in all there are 11 Dodgson children, and throughout his life Charles remains close to his brothers and sisters. Life at the secluded parsonage, a mile and a half from the little village of less than 200 inhabitants, necessarily centers around the family, in which Charles apparently spends what then would be considered a conventional middle-class childhood.

1843   The family moves to Croft, a town in Yorkshire, where the elder Dodgson becomes the rector of the Anglican parish. Living at Croft Rectory marks a great change for the family, providing them with a much better income, a more commodious house, and a richer social life than they had at Daresbury. Young Charles plays a major role in family entertainments—organizing amateur theatricals, devising whimsical games, and editing a series of little magazines intended for family circulation, among them *The Rectory Umbrella* (ca. 1849–53, published in 1932). The subversive parodies, ludicrous distortions and juxtapositions, and comic cruelty of these amateur magazines prefigure the distinctive Carrollian humor made famous by the *Alice* books. For example, in the first of these small magazines, *Useful and Instructive Poetry* (ca. 1845, published in 1954), young Charles parodies children's copy-book maxims typical of the era:

*This chronology contains only a small portion of the many works published under the names Charles Lutwidge Dodgson and Lewis Carroll.

Learn well your grammar,
And never stammer. . . . [a number of the Dodgson
   children stammered, including Charles]
Eat bread with butter.
Once more, don't stutter . . . .
Starve your canaries.
Believe in fairies. . . .

1844–1846   Leaves home to begin his formal education at Richmond Grammar School, 10 miles from Croft, where he demonstrates outstanding academic ability, especially in mathematics, his father's favorite subject.

1846–1850   Attends Rugby, one of England's foremost public (i.e., private) boarding schools, where he continues to be a first-rate scholar, but where he is also unhappy because of his shyness, his embarrassing (lifelong) stammer, and his aversion to the rough sports emphasized at Rugby.

1850   On 23 May matriculates at Christ Church College, Oxford, his father's alma mater and his own residence for the rest of his life. Again, he is an excellent student, winning academic prizes and honors, especially in mathematics.

1851   His mother dies suddenly on 26 January at age 47. He relieves his sorrow with even more strenuous schoolwork.

1852   Is nominated on 24 December to a studentship of Christ Church, a quasi-teaching position at Oxford, which he can retain for a lifetime so long as he remains unmarried and proceeds to holy orders (priesthood) in the Anglican church.

1854   Begins keeping a diary, which he continues meticulously until two weeks before his death in 1898. His diaries (first published in 1953) provide many insights into his life and art; unfortunately, four volumes, including the first, are missing. He is also throughout his lifetime a prolific and inventive letter writer (his Register of Letters Received and Sent was begun when he was 29 and recorded 98,721 letters). Among the many letters that have survived are numerous ones to a host of little-girl friends, some manifesting characteristic Carrollian humor, many manifesting unusual warmth and sensitivity to children.

1854–1856   Begins publishing his poetry and comic fiction in various periodicals, including *The Whitby Gazette, The Comic Times,* and *The Train.*

1854   Receives B.A. on 18 December. Within weeks, begins teaching private pupils in mathematics.

1855   Is named sublibrarian of Christ Church on 14 February. In July, starts keeping a kind of scrapbook, *Mischmasch* (published in 1932), in which he pastes or copies selections from his published and unpublished work. *Mischmasch* includes a "Stanza of Anglo-Saxon Poetry," which is ultimately expanded into what becomes the world's most famous nonsense poem, "Jabberwocky" of *Through the Looking-Glass* (1872). In the autumn begins his duties as a mathematical lecturer of Christ Church College, a post he retains until 1881; and in October is made a "Master of the House" in honor of the appointment of the new dean of Christ Church, Henry George Liddell, father of Alice Pleasance Liddell, the "Alice" of the *Alice* books.

1856   In contributions to *The Train,* first uses the pseudonym "Lewis Carroll," the name with which he will sign most of his published fiction and poetry for the rest of his life. In the spring buys his first camera, beginning a career as one of the period's most important amateur portrait photographers, especially of young girls. Meanwhile, his official profession of teaching mathematics is going from bad to worse; he has trouble even maintaining classroom discipline. On 25 April, in the dean's garden, meets (apparently for the first time) and attempts to photograph the dean's three daughters, including Alice Pleasance Liddell. In his diary entry for this day he writes, "The three little girls were in the garden most of the time, and we became excellent friends. . . . I mark this day with a white stone" (a comment he often uses to record a special occasion).

1857   Receives his M.A. on 5 February. Continues to make friends with numerous little girls and to attend many plays in London, two of his lifelong passions. By means, primarily, of the contacts afforded by his photography, he develops friendships with numerous children as well as literary and theatrical celebrities, including Ruskin, Tennyson, D. G. Rossetti, and Ellen Terry, the greatest English actress of the period.

1861   Is ordained deacon by Samuel Wilberforce, Bishop of Oxford, on 22 December. Although he remains a devout Anglican all his life, even preaching sermons occasionally, he never goes on to take holy orders for the priesthood, a violation of the terms of his college studentship that Dean Liddell apparently chooses to overlook.

1862   On 4 July Dodgson and Robinson Duckworth (later Canon) row up the Isis River from Oxford with the three young daughters of Dean Liddell (Alice is now 10) for an outing on which

Dodgson tells (probably for the first time) his extemporaneous accounts of Alice's underground adventures. At the end of the day, Alice begs him to write the story out for her, which he begins to do the next morning.

1863   Finishes the text for *Alice's Adventures under Ground*. On 10 February turns back to the 4 July 1862 diary entry that includes "Duckworth and I made an expedition *up* the river to Godstowe with the three Liddells" and adds this remark: "on which occasion I told them the fairy-tale of *Alice's Adventures Underground*, which is now finished (as to the text) though the pictures are not yet nearly done."

1863   Revises and expands the 18,000-word *under Ground* into the 35,000-word book we know today as *Alice's Adventures in Wonderland*. Between June and October Dodgson's friendship with the Liddell children is broken off inexplicably.

1864   Writes in his diary 12 May, "During these last few days I have applied in vain for leave to take the children on the river, i.e., Alice, Edith, and Rhoda: but Mrs. Liddell will not let *any* come in future—rather superfluous caution." On 5 April John Tenniel, a distinguished book illustrator and the leading political cartoonist of *Punch* magazine, accedes to Carroll's request to illustrate the *Alice* book, already accepted for publication by Macmillan and Company. On 28 June Dodgson chooses the title *Alice's Adventures in Wonderland*, after toying with other titles like "Alice's Hour in Elfland." On 26 November Alice Liddell receives as a Christmas gift the beautiful manuscript, *Alice's Adventures under Ground*, meticulously hand-printed and illustrated by Dodgson (this manuscript volume, sold in 1928 to an American for $50,000—the highest price ever paid up to that date for a book manuscript—by the original Alice Liddell, then 76 years old, is now back in England, in the British Library).

1865   In June, 2,000 copies of *Alice's Adventures in Wonderland* are printed by the Clarendon Press; and on 4 July a special white, vellum-bound presentation copy is sent to Alice Liddell at the deanery, exactly three years after the celebrated expedition to Godstowe. In July Tenniel expresses dissatisfaction with the printing of the pictures. On 2 August Dodgson writes in his diary, "Finally decided on the re-print of *Alice*, and that the first 2,000 shall be sold as waste paper." (The unbound sheets of this first edition are sold to D. Appleton and Company, New York publishers who issue the book in America in 1866.) The second edition, dated 1866, comes out in November 1865, and

Dodgson pronounces it "very *far* superior to the old, and in fact a perfect piece of artistic printing."

1866   *Alice's Adventures in Wonderland* is an immediate success with both children and adults, at first primarily because it breaks with the strong tradition of didactic, moralistic books for children. By August, Dodgson is already considering French and German translations of the book.

1867   From 12 July to 14 September tours the Continent and visits Russia with Henry Parry Liddon, his Christ Church friend and colleague since the mid-1850s and an influential churchman on a mission to encourage a reunion between the Eastern Orthodox church and the Church of England. This is Dodgson's only trip outside England. In the autumn, publishes an *Elementary Treatise on Determinants,* one of many mathematical works he produces (usually as "Charles L. Dodgson") throughout his career.

1868   In June Dodgson's father dies, an event he later describes as "the greatest blow that has ever fallen on my life." Now, as head of the family, he buys a new home for his sisters in Guildford, near Oxford. He moves into commodious rooms in Tom Quad, where he lives for the rest of his life. Maintaining his rooms with characteristic precision and order, the methodical Dodgson, despite his shyness, is host to many visitors throughout his life, especially little girls he often entertains with his large collections of games, puzzles, toys, music boxes, and gadgets—as well as his photography.

1869   In January publishes (under the pseudonym Lewis Carroll) *Phantasmagoria and Other Poems,* a collection of 13 comic poems and 13 serious poems. French and German translations of *Alice's Adventures in Wonderland* appear, the first of thousands of translations in the nineteenth and twentieth centuries into hundreds of different languages.

1871   In December *Through the Looking-Glass and What Alice Found There* (dated 1872) is published and is an immediate success with a wide reading public.

1872   Publishes *The New Belfry,* one of the first of a number of conservative pamphlets, some serious and some comic, about Oxford controversies that he publishes privately and anonymously throughout his lifetime.

1875   Publishes *Some Popular Fallacies about Vivisection* (signed Lewis Carroll), a pamphlet that attempts to discredit vivisection, a practice that concerns him for many years.

1876   29 March: Publishes *The Hunting of the Snark,* illustrated by Henry Holiday. This becomes the most celebrated Carroll book, after the *Alice*s, and one of the world's great works of absurd humor.

1879   Publishes *Euclid and His Modern Rivals,* one of his best known mathematical works, combining serious argument with an amusing Carrollian style (signed Charles L. Dodgson).

1880   Suddenly and inexplicably abandons photography, for 25 years a beloved avocation in which he has risen to professional eminence. Some biographers conjecture that this sudden event was precipitated by Dodgson's troubles with mothers whose daughters he wanted to photograph in the nude (several such nude photographs survive). His income from the sale of his books (especially the *Alice*s) has reached such proportions that Dodgson proposes a one-third cut in his 300-pound studentship salary, thus allowing him more time for his many literary projects in what he views as his last years of life.

1881   On 18 October writes to Dean Liddell informing him of his intention to resign his lectureship. Only two students out of nine attend his last mathematics class on 30 November. He is full of plans for books to be written in his retirement.

1882   Is elected curator of the Christ Church Common Room, a post he holds until 1892, on 8 December. An onerous task (before the age of professional college administrators and in a college where many of the discriminating dons make their homes), the curatorship includes responsibility for the selection, purchase and storage of such items as food and wines, coal, newspapers, stationery, and furniture, as well as for the hiring and payment of the servants. Dodgson takes up the job with characteristic fastidiousness, industry, and pleasure in complexity—and produces mountains of meticulous letters as well as several serio-comic Oxford pamphlets related to his many duties as curator.

1883   On 6 December publishes *Rhyme? and Reason?,* a collection of poems, most already published, and including all of *The Hunting of the Snark.*

1886   In November publishes, with the permission of Alice Liddell (now Mrs. Hargreaves), a photographic facsimile of his 1862–63 manuscript book, *Alice's Adventures under Ground.*

1886–1887   Publishes *The Game of Logic,* a game designed to teach children the basic principles of formal logic with humorous Carrollian examples.

1889   In October publishes *The Nursery "Alice,"* a condensed, simplified, and rather patronizing version of *Alice's Adventures in Wonderland,* containing 20 colored enlargements of Tenniel's original *Wonderland* illustrations. In November also publishes another children's book, the massive (400 pages) *Sylvie and Bruno,* an almost plotless fairy tale laced with serious religious and scientific matters and with heavy doses of embarrassing sentimentality, but also here and there with isolated examples of effective Carrollian humor.

1893   On 29 December publishes *Sylvie and Bruno Concluded,* a lengthy (423 pages) continuation of the first *Sylvie and Bruno* volume, in the same style, with some humorous treatments of such subjects as physics and politics.

1896   Publishes *Symbolic Logic,* a serious attempt to popularize formal logic and accuracy of thought and, according to some twentieth-century experts, an important forerunner of modern symbolic logic.

1897   Publishes his finally revised edition of *Alice's Adventures in Wonderland,* now a world-famous classic.

1898   Dies of bronchitis 14 January at 2:30 P.M. at his sisters' home, "The Chestnuts" in Guildford. Is buried in the Guildford cemetery under a white cross inscribed simply "Revd. Charles Lutwidge Dodgson" and under that "(Lewis Carroll) Fell Asleep Jan. 14, 1898. Aged 65 years."

ALICE'S ADVENTURES IN WONDERLAND
and
THROUGH THE LOOKING-GLASS

Nonsense, Sense, and Meaning

LITERARY AND
HISTORICAL CONTEXT

1.

The *Alice* Books and Lewis Carroll's World

This study rests on the premise that appreciating Lewis Carroll's *Alice* books (1862–72) does not require extensive knowledge of their historical setting. Their continuous popularity among large and varied audiences for the past 120 years shows how accessible they are: lay readers seeking to experience and understand their power need not acquire a vocabulary of outdated words and unfamiliar historical facts, of obsolete concepts and attitudes. This does not mean, however, that the *Alices* are unrelated to their original cultural matrix: like all other artifacts, they are products of their era, bearing inscriptions of numerous transactions with the material and ideological contexts from which they first emerged. So while the *Alices* provide readers with what often seems a glorious escape from time and place—from historical context itself—some of their most memorable effects depend on tangible connections to their specific historical milieu.

However, because Lewis Carroll's world of the 1860s bears many resemblances to middle-class life in developed countries today, these connections are often relatively easy to understand and appreciate In their daily lives, Carroll and his first readers experienced intimately the changes produced by industrialism, laissez-faire capitalism, and limited representative democracy, and familiar features of that familiar context often appear in Alice's dream fantasies. The sense of life in an unregulated, rapidly expanding, free-market economy in a secularized and fragmented society whose various power arrangements, competing classes, goals, and values are rapidly changing in response to numerous technological, economic, demographic, and political changes is a sense of life we share with Carroll and his contemporaries. Indeed, because the Victorian bourgeoisie were experiencing our world in its nascent state and because many of them still knew directly and yearned earnestly for another, much slower-paced, more coherent world of serene certainties and secure social values, their reactions to such unprecedented change are frequently fresher, more passionate, and more vivid than are our comparatively blasé or resigned reactions to similar cultural phenomena.

When, for example, Alice discovers herself in a looking-glass railroad carriage (L, chapter 3), modern readers should find the scene's references to the details of public rail travel generally familiar. Even more familiar will be the scene's hyperbolic representations of time as an industrial construct, of time's ridiculous but actual connection with money and by extension with a frenzied getting-and-spending capitalist system—a dream subject directly relevant to the wide-awake anxieties suffered by Victorians as a result of the rapid expansion of consumerism, a cash economy, machinery, and mechanically measured time as dominant forces in their daily lives. Taken together, the extremely fast-paced Alice adventures caricature a paradigmatic shift in the very conception of time, a shift greatly accelerated in the nineteenth century by major discoveries in astronomy, geology, and biology, and by technological achievements like the rapid development during the first half of the Victorian age of the factory system, railways, steamships, and telegraph lines—four of the period's many contributions to commerce, transportation, and communications that radically changed the relations between time and space and the way people live in them (a central topic of the Alices).

The rapidity of change occurring almost everywhere during the period, the dizzying pace of life in a multifarious, mechanized mass society is reflected in Alice's fast-paced, crowded, discontinuous dream adventures. So too is the sense of speedy motion, not for the sake of progress toward a definitive goal, but simply for its own sake. Thus, the Red Queen's frequently quoted response to Alice's assertion that "in *our* country . . . you'd generally get to somewhere else—if you ran very fast for a long time as we've been doing" is especially relevant to the empty bustle of urban existence in Carroll's mid-Victorian England, an England suddenly coming to question its own faith in inevitable progress and the benefits of mechanical invention. "Now, *here*," says the Queen, "it takes all the running *you* can do, to keep in the same place" (*L*, 127).

> "Tickets, please!" said the [railway] Guard, putting his head in at the window. In a moment everyone was holding out a ticket: they were about the same size as the people, and quite seemed to fill the carriage.
> "Now then! Show your ticket, child!" the Guard went on, looking angrily at Alice. And a great many voices all said together ("like the chorus of a song," thought Alice), "Don't keep him waiting, child! Why, his time is worth a thousand pounds a minute!" (*L*, 129–30)

The anxious dream-satire of the *Looking-Glass* railway scene is directed, in part, at the improbable regimentation and commercialization of what was until then considered beyond such strict mechanical control and quantitative measurement. In Alice's dream of the railroad carriage, time and space are measurable by a new mechanized, monetary standard. Money, not inherent worth, now determines value; now "time is money" (the insubstantial "smoke alone," according to the awe-inspired consumers in Alice's carriage, "is worth a thousand pounds a puff!" [*L*, 130]). Tickets the size of human beings represent with surreal clarity the way various social and commerical institutions, like mass transportation, had during Carroll's childhood and youth grown to the point of dwarfing, dominating, even crowding out the people they were meant to serve, quickly turning the recent masters of the machines into the machines' clockwork "chorus" of harried, cramped, but worshipful servants—a process that deeply troubled many intellectuals among Carroll's earnest contemporaries, including the famous literary prophets of social disaster, Thomas Carlyle, Matthew Arnold, and Carroll's friend John Ruskin.

The frantic railway scene is but one example of the numerous allusions in the *Alices* to the mechanization, commodification, and acceleration that were transforming Victorian life. The first character Alice meets is the harried White Rabbit, a desperate slave to his watch and busy schedule. Moreover, many of the humanoid creatures in her adventures are actually mechanical things playing mechanical parts— cards, chessmen, set figures from traditional nursery rhymes—inflexible cogs in an unprogressive, incomprehensible but perpetual, all-consuming social mechanism.

In the world's great age of machinery, England was the very center of the Industrial Revolution, "the world's workshop" and the epitome of the modern shift from manual to mechanical labor. Effecting an enormous transformation in the quality of everyday life, this triumph of materialism and machinery was celebrated by many Victorians, especially those in the newly rising classes; but it was at the same time often deplored in a variety of Victorian literary texts, perhaps most powerfully in the fantastic, often bitter satire of Charles Dickens (one of Carroll's favorite authors and popular among all literate classes), who in a series of best-selling novels in the 1850s and 1860s created a large, funny, but macabre gallery of caricatured Victorians dehumanized by the system into manufactured, automatic, scurrying *things*.

CULTURAL ANARCHY

In the same years as the publication of Alice's anarchic adventures, Matthew Arnold, the leading literary/cultural critic of his time, warned in his most famous work, *Culture and Anarchy* (1869), of the ways the British worship of machinery was quickly leading to anarchy: "Faith in machinery is . . . our besetting danger; often in machinery most absurdly disproportioned to the end which this machinery, if it is to do any good at all, is to serve; but always in machinery, as if it had a value in and for itself. What is freedom but machinery? What is population but machinery? What is coal but machinery? what are railroads but machinery? what is wealth but machinery? what are, even, religious organizations but machinery?"[1]

For many conservative, establishment figures like Arnold and his fellow Oxford don Carroll (both were also graduates of Rugby as well as sons of upper-middle-class Church of England clergymen), "machinery" could be a heavily fraught symbol for the loss of traditional humane values, for cultural anarchy, even for imminent political revolution:

> For a long time . . . the strong feudal habits of subordination and deference continued to tell upon the working class. The modern spirit has now almost entirely dissolved those habits, and the anarchical tendency of our worship of freedom in and for itself, of our superstitious faith, as I say, in machinery, is becoming very manifest. More and more, because of this our blind faith in machinery, because of our want of light to look beyond machinery to that end for which machinery is valuable, this and that man, and this and that body of men, all over the country, are beginning to assert and put into practice an Englishman's right to do what he likes; his right to march where he likes, enter where he likes, hoot as he likes, threaten as he likes, smash as he likes. All this, I say, tends to anarchy. (Arnold, 76)

The Victorian mechanical revolution, then, was part of a broad context of interdependent revolutions—intellectual, scientific, economic, political, social, religious, artistic—in an age of revolution. The revolution in biological theory, generally attributed to Darwin but actually begun earlier in the century, generated among Victorian intellectuals a frightening vision of "Nature, red in tooth and claw" (Tennyson, *In Memoriam*)[2] and of themselves as no more than one of countless, dispensable species in an inescapable biological mechanism governed (like laissez-faire capitalism) by survival-of-the-fittest instincts. Soon, numbers of earnest thinkers were seeing themselves and their fellows as mere selfish, appetitive apes thinly disguised as altruistic, humane, re-spectable Victorian ladies and gentlemen. This materialistic, God-less vision profoundly affected philosophical thought, religious belief, and political action—almost every area of social concern. Moreover, the revolutionary notion of inevitable class warfare—linked to nineteenth-century evolutionary theory, mass industrialization, laissez-faire eco-nomics, a large and growing proletariat, urbanization, cheap labor, unionization, cycles of inflation and depression, and devastating pov-erty in the midst of immense wealth—created for the elite, privileged, once-secure class of Arnold and Carroll the frightening prospect of literal anarchy and revolution. (Friedrich Engels's *The Condition of the Working Class in England in 1844* was based on firsthand observations of the deplorable conditions of workers in Manchester; with Karl Marx, Engels published *The Communist Manifesto* in 1848, translated into English in 1850.) Despite several Parliamentary Reform Bills dur-ing the period that gradually granted voting rights and some political power to larger, less privileged segments of the population, and despite other social reforms that ameliorated the worst horrors of an unregu-lated capitalist system, England seemed for much of the period danger-ously close to the political upheavals that had periodically rocked Eu-rope since the days of the bloody French Revolution. "The fear of revolution," as one leading Victorian scholar puts it, "had almost be-come part of the collective unconscious."[3]

A WORLD TURNED UPSIDE DOWN

These revolutionary tendencies of the period and the anxieties they provoked often lie close to the surface of Alice's dreams. In a sense, the *Alice* books are about revolution in that they present a funny but anxious vision of an entire middle-class world turned upside down: two topsy-turvy, "backwards" places where the sensible child of the master class acts as servant, and the crazy servants act as masters; where inanimate, manufactured playing cards and chessmen have seized control, giving rude orders to a real, live, polite human representative of the ruling class that had but recently manipulated them as inert counters in games of her class's devising; where time itself will no longer "behave" its erstwhile governors so that in the Mad Tea-Party it is always six o'clock (quitting time for many factory workers); where the old, comfortable, seemingly unchanging social fabric has been so unravelled that each atomized creature now lives in its own, completely self-centered, disconnected world, freed from the fabricated "rules" and traditions of bourgeois community, rank and order.

The once sacrosanct, relatively static class system that had served, primarily, the interests of a small minority of privileged Anglican gentlemen like Arnold and Carroll was therefore deeply threatened by change in an increasingly materialistic, competitive society, increasingly driven by mechanical innovation and the volatile, mechanistic standards of the market. For adherents of the bourgeois ethos like Carroll or like his adored heroine Alice, daughter of Dean Liddell of Christ Church College, Oxford, such revolutions represented a threat to personal identity itself: "What *will* become of me?" (W, 28) is a question Alice often asks, in various forms, throughout her adventures. Given its historical context, the question deals with far more than her physical nature: it carries for her class broad and sinister implications. So too does Gilbert and Sullivan's hilarious comment on this social aspect of their revolutionary age as that age drew to a close: "When every one is somebodee, / Then no one's anybody!" (*The Gondoliers*, 1889).

Carroll's mature lifetime was passed in an age of burgeoning technology that rapidly increased the spread of new material goods, ideas, and ways of doing things; of unprecedented population concentrations in cities; of enormous factories and serious environmental pollution; of great shifts in the distribution of wealth and power; of Karl Marx's *Das Kapital* (the first volume, written in England, appeared in 1867) and the rise of English socialism; and, in general, of the zenith and incipient decline of the bourgeois hegemony in politics and culture. Beyond England's shores, it was also the heyday of the British Empire—arguably the greatest empire the world has ever known, but an empire already threatened by violent revolutions against imperialism as well as by peaceful but irreversible evolutions toward colonial independence (Canada, for instance, became essentially self-governing in 1867).

It was, moreover, the period of Freud's youth (Freud was 13 years old when *Wonderland* was first translated into German in 1869), of impressionism in the arts, of a growing fascination with dreams and other workings of the inner life—with what Walter Pater, the age's leading aesthetician, characterized just three years after the publication of *Alice's Adventures in Wonderland* as the individual "mind keeping as a solitary prisoner its own dream of a world."[4] At the same time, it was also the period that witnessed among the middle-classes a wide dissemination of earlier Romantic views of child psychology and of the child as the innocent, near-divine "father of the Man." These views, in turn, fostered a burgeoning body of children's literature (like the *Alices*) aimed at nurturing young readers' precious innate creative imaginations rather than beating out their natural savagery or filling their blank-tablet minds with didactic, cautionary tales.

It was, in addition, an age of intensified sexism and misogyny (critic and reformer John Ruskin's notorious "Of Queens' Gardens" [1864–71] is often cited as the paradigm of the patriarchal "woman's place in the home" and "on the pedestal" ideology that permeated the culture). But at the same time it witnessed the public emergence of successful, celebrated women intellectuals, among them the Brontës, Elizabeth Gaskell, George Eliot, Harriet Martineau, and Elizabeth Barrett Browning. And it was the first age of organized, revolutionary feminism—a feminism that in some ways overshadows that of our own period (John Stuart Mill's *On the Subjection of Women,* a major philosophical formulation of modern feminism, was published in 1869).

Carroll's contemporaries also experienced a revolutionary crisis of faith perhaps unparalleled in modern history. Not only was the period plagued by bitter, destructive sectarianism among warring Christian denominations, it was also an age in which many of the best minds had already lost all religious conviction. It is of course no coincidence that in his 1869 indictment of his materialistic, mechanistic society, Arnold repeatedly uses such terms as *faith, religious,* and *worship.* Newly secularized, scientized England was, as Arnold suggests in a celebrated 1855 poem about faith and doubt, "wandering between two worlds, one dead, / One powerless to be born."[5] For Arnold and many other mid-Victorian thinkers, the fear was that England, now bereft of its "dead" world of a common religious faith, an established church, and a secure system of mystified bourgeois values, was quickly becoming a totally secular political entity, nothing more than a collection of self-serving factions and individuals lacking any true vitality, any agreed-on center of transcendent belief and ethical principles. As Arnold writes in "Dover Beach" (1867),

> The Sea of Faith
> Was once, too, at the full, and round earth's shore
> Lay like the folds of a bright girdle furl'd.
> But now I only hear
> Its melancholy, long, withdrawing roar,
> Retreating, to the breath
> Of the night-wind, down the vast edges drear
> And naked shingles of the world.[6]

Soon, it seemed, England would be merely a free-floating political aggregate held together by nothing more glorious than money or (enlightened) self-interest, devoid of its once-cherished cultural and spiritual landmarks—a godless place not unlike the chaotic underground into which poor Alice falls in her first adventure, or the "backwards" world she discovers just behind the comforting bourgeois looking-glass.

VICTORIAN EARNESTNESS

Victorians are often noted, sometimes ridiculed, for their irrepressible optimism and earnestness. Despite the grave doubts generated by the massive revolutionary changes that characterized their age, many of them continued to believe passionately in progress and in the efficaciousness of their earnest efforts to make their world better. Arnold himself, as if obeying Thomas Carlyle's Calvinist injunctions to dispel doubt by hard work in the concrete world, became in middle age a reforming commissioner of public education. In earnest do-it-yourself manuals like *Self-Help* (1859), *Lives of the Engineers* (1861–62), *Thrift* (1875), and *Duty* (1880), Samuel Smiles became one of the period's best-selling authors by preaching to the lower-middle and working classes a no-nonsense, humorless gospel of personal industry and unabashed get-ahead, commercial success.

But Victorians also knew how to make fun of their own earnestness, their middle-class reverence for work, money, and social respectability, as well as numerous other foibles of their complex, disturbing world. A number of the writers cited here—Carlyle, Dickens, and Gilbert and Sullivan most obviously; the Brontës, Eliot, and Arnold in more subtle ways—are noteworthy for their humorous treatments of the most serious social issues of their day. Victorian literature includes a wide variety of other writers who showed their age how to laugh at itself—among them, William Makepeace Thackeray, Edward Lear, George Meredith, Anthony Trollope, Samuel Butler, and the young George Bernard Shaw. The *Alice* books, like their earnest and very respectable author, the Reverend Charles Lutwidge Dodgson (alias Lewis Carroll), thus fit for another reason rather predictably into their historical context—an age of great comedy made in spite and at the expense of great earnestness. It should come as no surprise that the period ends with another earnest Victorian making wonderful, irreverent fun of respectability and earnestness, putting Victorianism in its final place, as he so often did, with epigrammatic and telling wit. Even in its title, Oscar Wilde's play *The Importance of Being Earnest* (1895) sounds the keynote of this admirably earnest age of revolution, bourgeois anxiety, and playful laughter.

2

The Importance of the *Alice* Books
and the Search for Their Meaning

Curiouser and curiouser!

Two of the most popular and durable classics in modern literature, Lewis Carroll's *Alice's Adventures in Wonderland* (1865) and *Through the Looking-Glass and What Alice Found There* (1872) also rank among literary history's most puzzling curiosities. Translated thousands of times[1] into scores of languages from Swahili to Swedish, from modern Czech to Mandarin Chinese, these brief volumes full of nursery rhymes, silly puns, and playful jokes written to amuse middle-class Victorian children are—along with the King James Bible and the plays of Shakespeare—the most quoted works ever written in English. Carroll's funny and confusing dream fantasies told in the simple vocabulary of a child have become for millions of adults around the world (many of whom have not actually read them) a revered institution, a cultural icon treasured as a repository of clear thoughts, profound insights, and enduring wisdom. No day passes without press accounts of prominent writers, film directors and artists, leading scientists, politicians, philosophers and religious figures alluding seriously to the *Alices*—as if these apparently slight and silly books somehow convey fundamental truths for our age.

Despite many skillful attempts over the past 70 years to account for the durability of the *Alice* books and their relevance to life in widely diverse cultures, a fully satisfying explanation of their "meaning" and of their perennial hold over adult imaginations continues to elude even the shrewdest scholars and critics. Indeed, regardless of the good sense the books make for countless readers, the *Alices* are also often cited as prime models of "nonsense," a genre whose success depends upon a *lack* of applicable "meaning"—a liberating and delicious indeterminacy, an immunity from the usual demands upon classics to make good sense about real life.

Alice, in many ways an ordinary bourgeois child of her own era, is often celebrated today as a universal figure of heroic dimensions. In spite of her class- and time-bound prejudices, her frightened fretting and childish, abject tears, her priggishness and self-assured ignorance, her sometimes blatant hypocrisy, her general powerlessness and confusion, and her rather cowardly readiness to abandon her struggles at the ends of the two adventures—in spite of all these apparent shortcomings, many readers look up to Alice as a mythic embodiment of self-control, perseverance, bravery, and mature good sense.

There is also the curious question of Alice's own questionable curiosity. She darts down the rabbit hole and climbs through the looking-glass impelled by a seemingly insatiable desire for new knowledge, "never once considering," we are told at the beginning of her first underground adventure, "how in the world she was to get out again" (W, 8). In most episodes, her refreshing sense of wonder drives the plot, keeping readers racing with her from one adventure to another. But the charm of that daring, effervescent curiosity is frequently vitiated by her ridiculous self-assurance and by her alacrity to leave off questioning at precisely the moment when useful answers might emerge from the apparent void in which she travels. Thus, her curiosity seems to lead her nowhere, and she ends her adventures no better off, it seems, than when she began. In fact, if the *Alices* teach anything at all, their lesson might be that Alice's curiosity is, as the Cheshire Cat says, merely an act of insanity, a mad choice to "go among mad people" (W, 51).

ALICE'S CREATOR

Adding to the complications of such fictional curiosities are a number of curious facts about their author. It is important to note, for example, that Charles Lutwidge Dodgson (1832–98), a shy, celibate, conservative, and rather obscure Oxford mathematics don, never publicly acknowledged that he was also Lewis Carroll, the creator of the enormously successful, hilariously subversive dream-story *Alices*, as well as *The Hunting of the Snark* and other wildly playful imaginative works during a productive but semisecret literary career. In fact, throughout the decades of fame and fortune that the *Alices* and the name "Lewis Carroll" enjoyed during his lifetime, while he readily acknowledged his pen name among his friends (and especially among the scores of little girls he cherished all his life and to whom he wrote wonderfully affectionate, absurdly comic letters signed Lewis Carroll), the Reverend Mr. Dodgson strenuously persisted in public denials of any connection with these celebrated books with which he took such pains and in which he took such personal pride. Hence, he regularly returned strangers' mail addressed to him as Lewis Carroll with a printed leaflet that asserted, "Mr. Dodgson is so frequently addressed by strangers on the quite unauthorized assumption that he claims or at any rate acknowledges the authorship of books not published under his name, that he has found it necessary to print this, once for all, as an answer to all such applications. He neither claims nor acknowledges any connection with any pseudonym, or with any book that is not published under his own name."[2]

The abundant evidence of this carefully maintained separation between Charles Lutwidge Dodgson, conventional churchman and scrupulous devotee of logic and order, and Lewis Carroll, irreverent, playful celebrant of fantastic mayhem, suggests one important basis for the odd, enduring power of the *Alices*. The extremely precise, meticulous Dodgson, whose obsessive efforts to order the details of his daily affairs often bordered on the pathological, created behind his Lewis Carroll mask two of the most disorderly places in all Western art—the mad underground world of *Wonderland* and the puzzling backwards world of *Through the Looking-Glass,* places so anarchic that a number of literary critics have read them as visions of universal chaos. However, the connections here between order and chaos, sober reality and playful dream, sentimental Charles Dodgson and satiric Lewis Carroll, and their connections, in turn, to the modern appeal of the *Alices* are not as easy to decode as they might seem. The process of decoding them, moreover, courts the interpretive dangers of any schematic, mechanical literary exegesis.

ANALYZING THE *ALICES*

Thus, the reader curious to understand more fully the *Alice* books faces a particularly daunting task. That task is even more daunting because the delicate comic spirit of Carroll's masterpieces characteristically resists rational explication: if explanations by their nature tend to spoil jokes, here they run the serious risk of destroying the matrix of Carroll's unique absurd humor—the fragile, subtle indefinableness on which the vitality of Carrollian comedy often depends.

On the other hand, the *Alices* present curious readers with a peculiarly attractive challenge. For if those readers succeed in finding some satisfactory answers to these questions about the books' meanings and methods, they succeed also in increasing their understanding of things well beyond Lewis Carroll and his great comic fantasies—things that impinge directly on their own lives, their own modes of understanding, their own "meaning" as human beings. For these so-called nonsensical adventures seem to suggest, as the reverence of innumerable adult readers and the commentaries of many astute critics attest, valuable responses to fundamental questions like "What is the meaning of *meaning?*" "Is meaning necessarily contingent and relative?" "How do we mean what we mean?" "What does it mean to exist? to be human?" or "What does it all mean?"

One possible reaction of course to such teasing but difficult questions about the meaning of the *Alices* is to dismiss the questions entirely: to declare that because the books have succeeded so well among so many millions of readers unequipped with and unhampered by rational explanations of their wide and deep appeal, questions about their ultimate meanings are unnecessary—or best left to the esoteric investigations of professional philosophers and literary theorists. The *Alices* have of course been enjoyed by many adult readers for the "pure" pleasures they provide, the emotional pleasures innocent of "meaning": fascinating, fearful, yet amusing stories read aloud by secure grown-ups; matter-of-fact narratives full of threatening episodes that end comfortably enclosed in the safe category of mere dreams. It could even be argued that dreams, despite the frequent claims of Freudian psychoanalysis, are often best left unanalyzed, left to work their dramatic therapies by mysterious, hidden ways.

Some readers might assume Carroll himself encourages such passive, unanalytic approaches to the "meaning" of his *Alices*, ending them as he does with the trite rhetorical question, "Life, what is it but a dream?" (*L*, 209). But in many other places he seems to suggest that, although grasping even the easiest meanings, the simplest relations between words and things (between "sounds" and "sense," as the Ugly Duchess puts it) is a terribly tricky business, it is one of the chief tasks we humans are made for. For the *Alices* provide many humorous yet serious commentaries on the means by which we mean what we say, the relations between the names of things and the things themselves. When, for example, the *Wonderland* March Hare tells Alice, "You should say what you mean," Alice replies hastily, "I do . . . at least I mean what I say—that's the same thing, you know." But the Mad Hatter knows better: "Not the same thing a bit!" he exclaims. "Why, you might just as well say that 'I see what I eat' is the same thing as 'I eat what I see'!" (*W*, 55). For despite their madness, the Hare and Hatter here seem to know a good deal more than Alice does about the relations between meaning and saying. Conversely, in *Looking-Glass* when Humpty Dumpty scornfully tells Alice that words—for most of us the principal medium of meaning—can mean anything ("When *I* use a word . . . it means just what I choose it to mean—neither more nor less"), Alice, who has matured a good deal since *Wonderland*, replies astutely, "The question is . . . whether you *can* make words mean so many different things" (*L*, 163). Years after the publication of the *Alice* books, Dodgson himself commented wryly, "Words mean more than we mean to express when we use them: so a whole book ought to mean a great deal more than the writer meant. So, whatever good meanings are in the book [*The Hunting of the Snark*], I'm very glad to accept as the meaning of the book."[3]

Regardless of these amusing but provocative Carrollian complications of "meaning," a hands-off, know-nothing approach to the meaning of the *Alice*s surely cannot satisfy the readers of this volume that purports to help them find that meaning. For although a few prominent Carroll scholars have derided almost all attempts at serious explication (Roger Lancelyn Green is perhaps the best example), among the many clumsy, wrongheaded, and downright incomprehensible attempts to interpret the books and their widespread appeal are a number of critical studies that do make good sense of the "nonsense," helping to satisfy in great part our curiosity about the meaning of these ostensibly silly stories that manifestly communicate serious truths about the human condition. (The Selected Bibliography is based, primarily, on those critical and scholarly works that are useful in this way.)

The basic assumptions informing the interpretations that follow, then, are 1) that the *Alice* books do make a lot of sense for a lot of mature readers, that "nonsense" is, for the most part, a misnomer for them; 2) that explication of the *Alice*s is not only desirable but entirely possible, even by general readers unequipped with specialized knowledge about such things as the Victorian age, Dodgson's life, or symbolic logic and mathematical theory; 3) that while the *Alice*s, like most other dreams, fantasies, and jokes, hardly ever say to us directly what they mean, and often say to us more than Carroll meant them to say, they most certainly mean seriously what they say; and 4) that although we can never hope to explain fully what these books mean or how they have secured their high place in the world's literature, our efforts in this regard can yield many important insights about them and about their meanings for us.

The following chapters are meant, among other things, to give critical readers a sampling of the many useful approaches they might take to questions of meaning in the *Alices*. They were, in essence, all published previously. Readers familiar with the originals will probably find little new—except perhaps the evidence that, in preparing this volume, I have discovered how those five separate pieces were, despite their differing topics and approaches, actually parts of a single, unfolding vision of the *Alices*, a vision that now confirms my first impressions of them as important books about the modern temper and the modern need for meaning.

In the introduction to her 1984 study, *Fantasy and Mimesis: Responses to Reality in Western Literature*, Kathryn Hume asserts, "Hemingway, in mimetic terms, says, 'this is what life is like.' In the metaphoric manner permitted by their fantasies, so do Kafka and Lewis Carroll."[4] To look carefully and critically at Carroll's great fantasies is, frequently, to look carefully and critically at an important metaphor of "what life is like." And although we cannot hope to achieve a simple, all-encompassing explanation of their inexhaustible meanings, we can expect, through a better understanding of their particular literary characteristics—often seeing in their metaphorical strategies *how* they mean in order to understand *what* they mean—to approach a more satisfying explanation of the curious relation they bear to life, to the common condition of the vast, enormously varied audience they continue to instruct and delight.

3

Critical Reception
of the *Alice* Books

The *Alice* books did well from the beginning. In his biography of his recently deceased and now world-famous uncle, Charles Lutwidge Dodgson, Stuart Dodgson Collingwood reported that the first critics of *Alice's Adventures in Wonderland* had been "loud in their praises. . . . [T]here was hardly a dissentient voice among them, and the reception which the public gave the book justified their opinion." Six months after Carroll's death, a *Pall Mall Gazette* poll of English readers' preferences in children's books placed *Alice's Adventures in Wonderland* first and *Through the Looking-Glass* in the top twenty.[1] Moreover, numerous North American editions and translations into a host of foreign languages during Carroll's lifetime attest to the books' immediate popularity abroad. By the end of the Victorian age they were international classics.

Until well into the twentieth century, however, the *Alice*s were seen almost exclusively as children's literature. Their popularity derived from the liberating imaginative experience they offered young readers reared on a dreary diet of unimaginative, "useful" texts devised to improve their minds, morals, and manners. Victorian children were delighted with these fresh, undidactic tales of adventure and fantasy: here were stories made, apparently, not for their edification, but for their entertainment. The *Alices* also offered child readers a realistic heroine with whom they could identify. Indeed, Alice's very first sentence in *Wonderland*—her introduction, so to speak, to the entire book—is a conspiratorial, ironic in-joke about utility addressed especially to child readers: "And what is the *use* of a book," she asks rhetorically, "without pictures or conversations?" (*W,* 7; my italics). *Wonderland*'s adult narrator soon joins Alice's conspiracy against prevailing trends in children's books, satirizing in this case the pedestrian (and sometimes gruesome) cautionary tales that made up a considerable portion of Victorian children's "recreational" reading:

> [Alice] had read several nice little stories about children who had got burnt, and eaten up by wild beasts, and other unpleasant things, all because they *would* not remember the simple rules their friends had taught them; such as, that a red-hot poker will burn you if you hold it too long; and that, if you cut your finger *very* deeply with a knife, it usually bleeds; and she had never forgotten that, if you drink much from a bottle marked "poison," it is almost certain to disagree with you, sooner or later. (*W,* 10–11)[2]

In the 1920s and 1930s, a number of prominent authors and literary critics discovered that the delightful *Alice* fantasies that had captivated their generation as children continued to engage them as adults, resonating with mature concerns and perplexities about existence, knowledge, human motivation, and society. The *Alices,* they found, frequently addressed issues beyond the comprehension and appreciation of even the most precocious child. They came to believe that Carroll had informed these "nonsense" books—whether consciously or unconsciously—with much sense. Soon, therefore, the *Alices* began to receive the sort of professional critical attention usually devoted to literature meant exclusively for grown-ups. It became evident that these seriocomic fantasies, ostensibly aimed at children, enjoyed a large and enthusiastic readership among adults. By 1930, Walter De La Mare, one of the leading English poets of his generation, could find many adults to agree with him that the books have "delights in them which only many years' experience of life can fully reveal."[3] And in 1932, Edmund Wilson, perhaps the most astute and hard-headed American literary critic of his day, complained that Carroll "deserves better" than the sentimental appreciations of previous critics, the works of "admirers . . . who revel in his delightfulness and cuteness but do not give him any serious attention." Moreover, other British and American critics were coming to agree with Wilson's contention that it was "the psychological truth of these books that lays its hold on us all," children and adults alike.[4]

FREUD AND ALICE

Given this growing recognition of the books' seriousness and of their powerful, moving psychological insights, it was inevitable that as the Freudian approach to artistic works became fashionable in intellectual circles of the 1930s and 1940s, the *Alices* would become prime texts for interpretation both by psychoanalytic literary critics and by professional psychoanalysts interested more in Carroll's putative pathology than in the philosophical meaning or literary dynamics of his texts. Reputedly composed more or less by free association, the books offered fertile ground for psychoanalytic interpretation, especially so since their author was a celibate, properly repressed Victorian gentleman, the conventional Reverend Charles Lutwidge Dodgson, who—somewhat like the Victorian Dr. Jeckyll with his Mr. Hyde—hid his connections with his extremely irreverent alter ego, the unconventional, zany children's author Lewis Carroll. The texts were, moreover, replete with primal scenes and overpowering, symbolic renditions of classic Freudian tropes (a vaginal rabbit hole and a phallic Alice, an amniotic pool of tears, hysterical mother figures and impotent father figures, threats of decapitation [castration], swift identity changes behind the comforting social facade of a looking-glass, etc.). Finally, each of the two books was at one and the same time dream, joke, and fantasy—an intriguing concentration in a single text of all the primary mechanisms, according to standard Freudian theory, for the mind to make manifest by means of displaced, surreptitious formulations the hidden, socially unacceptable desires and anxieties of the censored unconscious, particularly the repressed libido.

Until the present day, the psychoanalytic approach has played, in a variety of configurations, a leading role in *Alice* criticism. The theories of Sigmund and Anna Freud, Carl Jung, Erik Erikson, and most recently Jacques Lacan (as well as those of less prominent adapters of Freudian theory) have been applied to Carroll's life and literary fantasies by a host of literary critics and professional psychoanalysts with varying degrees of good judgment and interpretive success. One of the most influential applications of this approach occurred very early in an extremely provocative essay: William Empson's "*Alice in Wonderland:* The Child as Swain," the concluding chapter of Empson's celebrated book *Some Versions of the Pastoral* (1935). Despite Empson's assertion that "to make the dream-story from which *Wonderland* was elaborated seem Freudian one has only to tell it,"[5] however, his analysis, brief though it is, is by no means exclusively Freudian: it introduces, for example, a Marxist approach that even now, some 56 years later, has not been sufficiently explored by subsequent critics. As Carroll's most recent (1988) bibliographer states, "In 1935 Empson set the stage for serious scholarship on Carroll and introduced most of the major literary issues related to the character of Alice. In fact, he is cited so frequently by later scholars that his name has practically become a Carroll by-word."[6]

Among the many perceptive critical studies that depend on Freudian theory is one from the 1940s that continues to rank among the best critical biographies of Carroll—Florence Becker Lennon's *Victoria through the Looking-Glass: The Life of Lewis Carroll* (1945). Examining Carroll and his fictions in the light of bourgeois Victorian repression, Lennon's study continues to illuminate crucial elements in the *Alices*. The most thorough, strictly psychoanalytic analysis of Carroll's life was published in 1955 by the eminent professional psychoanalyst Phyllis Greenacre—*Swift and Carroll: A Psychoanalytic Study of Two Lives.*

ALICE AND THE VICTORIAN ERA

In recent years, generic and theoretical distinctions have tended to blur in academic discourse about literature. Former separations, for example, between children's and adult literature, between popular and high culture, between fantasy and realism, between Freudianism and Marxism, between literary criticism and cultural anthropology have come to seem arbitrary and forced. In this eclectic intellectual atmosphere, the *Alice* books have been increasingly valued by critics as crucial cultural artifacts that offer important clues to the dynamics of Victorian and post-Victorian thought, ideology, and behavior. They have been studied recently in connection with a wide variety of culturally and politically oriented issues like the ideology of empire and colonialism; gender, sex, and the ethos of modern patriarchal societies; the development of nineteenth- and twentieth-century conceptions and exploitations of childhood; modern ego psychology and constructions of the self; the psychosocial foundations of modern irony and comic art; and the impact of Darwinian theory on nineteenth- and twentieth-century thought. Because of their mixtures of literary forms, their combinations and fusions of sense and nonsense, and their elusive referentiality, the *Alice*s have also attracted a great deal of critical attention from theorists of literary structures and genres. In France, for example, where Western fashions in literary theory and critical practice are often launched, the *Alice*s have been favorite texts among literary theorists ever since they were hailed in the 1920s and 1930s as forerunners of modern surrealism, a genre particularly popular among French artists and intellectuals in the first half of the century.

In the past 60 years, several important historical and publishing events have spurred an increasing production of Carroll scholarship and criticism, most of it centered on the *Alice*s. The hundredth anniversary of Dodgson's birth in 1932 was the first such event: it occasioned an outpouring of biographical and critical essays (including some by eminent literary figures like G. K. Chesterton and Lord David Cecil) and several noteworthy books, one by Langford Reed—*The Life of Lewis Carroll*—a useful semicritical study that unfortunately overemphasizes the legitimate, but rather limited split-personality approach to Carroll and the *Alices*. Also in 1932, Columbia University mounted a major exhibition to commemorate the centenary; the festivities included the presentation of an honorary doctorate to Mrs. Alice P. Liddell Hargreaves (1852–1934), Carroll's original Alice, and a dedicatory speech by Columbia professor Harry Morgan Ayres, an eminent Old English scholar. Ayres expanded this speech into the book *Carroll's Alice* (1936), a brief but thought-provoking and witty discussion of the themes of education and growing up in Carroll's fictions. Since then many critics have pursued those pregnant themes with varying degrees of success.

DODGSON'S DIARIES AND LETTERS

IN 1953, *The Diaries of Lewis Carroll,* edited by Roger Lancelyn Green, were published for the first time, thus providing biographically oriented scholars and critics with important new information about Carroll and his *Alices*. Derek Hudson's dependable but rather uncritical and uninspiring biography, the first to use these published diaries, appeared in the following year. *The Letters of Lewis Carroll* in two volumes, meticulously edited by Morton N. Cohen, one of the world's most knowledgeable and prolific Carroll scholars, were published in 1979. Although neither of these collections is complete, the access they offer to the author's personal life has been invaluable to critics. One important effect of the publication of these and other primary biographical documents was to dispel the widespread but erroneous belief that Dodgson was a shy, stuttering, reclusive Oxford don, a pitiable, neurotic product of excessive bourgeois respectability whose only outlets for his deeply repressed playfulness and irreverence were the iconoclastic *Alice* books he wrote under an assumed name and his (childish) friendships with children. The diaries and letters reveal, in contrast, a generous, loving man who led a busy and fulfilling social and professional life, one whose personal communications were regularly leavened by the same "Carrollian" playfulness and wit that had made the

*Alice*s beloved by millions of readers around the world, whose wide circle of friends and acquaintances, besides the scores of little girls he adored, included a number of the most prominent artistic figures of the age (including the period's leading poet, Alfred Tennyson; its greatest portrait photographer, Julia Margaret Cameron; its favorite actress, Ellen Terry; its major painter-poet, Dante Gabriel Rossetti; Dante Gabriel's equally gifted sister, the poet Christina Rossetti; and its most important art critic, as well as one of its major social philosophers, John Ruskin). In the light of these newly available biographical data, the simplistic split-personality views of earlier Carroll biographers and critics became untenable. Similarly, views of the *Alice*s as strange nonsensical mutants in an age of earnestly sensible social consciousness have been steadily eroded by the growing numbers of studies demonstrating how these triumphs of comic free play also exemplify the profound questioning of reality and social norms that characterized the mainstream of nineteenth-century English literature.

COLLECTED CRITICISM

Another major impetus to Carroll scholarship and criticism has been the continual publication, since 1960, of annotated *Alice* and *Snark* editions and collections of interpretive essays by various Carroll experts. The most influential of the annotated editions is Martin Gardner's *The Annotated Alice* of 1960 (recently supplemented by Gardner's 1990 *More Annotated Alice*); also noteworthy is the 1982–83, two-volume, University of California Press *Alice*s annotated by James R. Kincaid. In the United States alone, at least six collections of critical essays have been published since my 1969 *Alice's Adventures in Wonderland: A Critical Handbook*. Among them are Donald Gray's indispensable Norton Critical Edition (1971, a revised edition to be published in 1992); Edward Guiliano's *Lewis Carroll Observed: A Collection of Unpublished Photographs, Drawings, Poetry, and New Essays* (1976), his *Lewis Carroll: A Celebration; Essays on the Occasion of the 150th Anniversary of the Birth of Charles Lutwidge Dodgson* (1982), and his and James R. Kincaid's *Soaring with the Dodo: Essays on Lewis Car-*

roll's Life and Art (1982); and Harold Bloom's *Modern Critical Views: Lewis Carroll* (1987). The most comprehensive of these anthologies is Robert Phillips's *Aspects of Alice: Lewis Carroll's Dreamchild as Seen through the Critics' Looking-Glasses, 1865–1971* (1971), which includes selections from most of the major Carroll critics since 1930 arranged in these categories: "Personal and Biographical"; "As Victorian and Children's Literature"; "Comparisons with Other Writers"; "Philosophical and Others"; "Church and Chess"; "Language, Parody and Satire"; "Freudian Interpretations"; "Jungian and Mythic"; and "Psychedelic."

Another significant development in *Alice* criticism occurred in the mid-1960s. Up until that point, critics invariably treated the two books as if they were a single text. This approach, as I argued in my 1966 essay, "Alice's Journey to the End of Night," seriously violated the artistic and thematic integrity of two closely related but very different works of art. Since then, many of the important critical studies have avoided lumping the two texts together, emphasizing instead their complementary but distinctly differing approaches to reality and literary form, as well as the progressive nature of Alice's development as she moves from the beginning of *Wonderland* to the end of *Looking-Glass*.

Because the *Alices* have attracted so much scholarly and critical attention since the 1960s, and because so many excellent aids to studying them have been published during these years, they have become extremely popular as required texts in college and university courses in a wide range of academic disciplines. This development has in turn increased the number of published interpretations to the point where even a cursory survey of only the most important critical discussions in the past 30 years would far exceed the space available here. Nevertheless, before concluding this outline of the books' critical reception, one more general approach deserves mention.

ALICE AND PHILOSOPHY

Because Dodgson was a professional, practicing mathematician and, furthermore, a thinker particularly interested in such branches of modern philosophical investigation as linguistics and symbolic logic (he published—sometimes under the name Lewis Carroll and sometimes under the name Charles Lutwidge Dodgson—a number of serious texts on these subjects), the *Alices* are now frequently interpreted as artistic representations of abstract philosophical issues (Peter Heath's *The Philosopher's Alice* [1974] is a valuable source for annotations on a wide range of philosophical questions treated by the *Alices*). Many critics examine the *Alices* in the light of abstract philosophical issues centered on what might be called "the meaning of meaning." (Again, one of the earliest attempts is still one of the best—Peter Alexander's 1951 "Logic and the Humour of Lewis Carroll.") Hence, provocative, influential books and essays have been published on the connections between the *Alice* books and mathematics, semiotics, semantics, and formal logic. And Carroll has been frequently cited as a brilliant precursor of such major twentieth-century philosophers as Henri Bergson, Bertrand Russell, and Ludwig Wittgenstein.

The fact that the most witty and elegant mathematical thought often need not "mean" anything, together with the growing academic interest in game theory, has provided the basis for several perceptive studies since the 1950s that interpret the *Alices* as pure, self-sufficient games. Biographical support for this approach can be found in Carroll's well-known fascination with games of all sorts—his publication, for example, of *A Game of Symbolic Logic,* his use of cards and chess as organizing elements in the two *Alices,* and his preoccupation with rules and all sorts of constructed ordering systems. This view of the *Alices* as abstract, self-contained, and nonreferential games is perhaps best exemplified by one of its earliest advocates, Elizabeth Sewell, whose 1952 study, *The Field of Nonsense,* elegantly argued that the *Alices,* like a game, have no meaning outside the arbitrary fields on which they are played. More recently, the topic has been explored usefully by Kathleen Blake in *Play, Games, and Sport: The Literary Works of Lewis Carroll* (1974).

Despite all the critical attention lavished on the *Alices* over the past 60 years, however, there still remain some serious gaps. For example, there have been (with, perhaps, a few debatable exceptions) no book-length critical studies in English devoted solely to the *Alices*—the result, perhaps, of the inherent difficulties associated with placing them in an established, recognized literary genre, or the daunting task of proposing to explain a kind of comedy that seems to defy and even ridicule explanations. Moreover, in spite of the admirable work of biographers like Lennon, Hudson, and most recently Anne Clark (*Lewis Carroll: A Biography,* 1979), there is not yet a really authoritative biography based on all the currently available primary materials (such as the diaries, letters, and important newly discovered items like the "suppressed" "Wasp in a Wig" episode from *Through the Looking-Glass* published for the first time in 1977 or Carroll's four photographs of nude girls first published in 1979). Carroll scholars eagerly await Morton N. Cohen's forthcoming biography, the culmination of some 25 years of assiduous scholarship. Other previously unavailable and unknown materials will no doubt appear in the future, shedding new light on the *Alices* (for example, the Lewis Carroll Society of North America is currently preparing for publication a six-volume series of all Carroll's pamphlets under the general editorship of Edward Guiliano).

ONGOING STUDIES

Rachel Fordyce ends the introduction to her *Lewis Carroll: A Reference Guide* (1988) with some helpful suggestions of important areas that still need further critical and scholarly attention: among them are connections between Carroll's fictions and folklore, relations between Alice's adventures and the quest tradition in literature, and the characteristics and responses of Carroll's original reading audience in England and elsewhere. A related topic that has received almost no attention revolves around the reasons for the appeal of the *Alices* among readers of particular socioeconomic classes. For the appeal of the books is curiously bifurcated: intellectuals look to them for incisive analyses of serious problems, enthusiastic amateurs for escapist nonsense. Many adult readers, especially the affluent and privileged, cherish the *Alices,* like *The Wind in the Willows,* as genteel, "meaningless" fantasies that offer a comforting vision of a mythic stable past, a refuge from the concrete problems of modern life—especially from responsibility for the failures of their social and political systems and the plight of their less fortunate fellow human beings. Moreover, from the earliest *Alice* studies until the present, arguments have been made by a small number of prominent Carroll scholars like Roger Lancelyn Green that the so-called nonsense of the *Alices* is truly nonsense and that any attempts at critical exegesis are in a sense sacrilegious violations of more or less holy, inexplicable texts. A study of the dynamics of this particular form of fetishism/escapism would focus on those "admirers" who, in Edmund Wilson's view, "revel in [Carroll's] delightfulness and cuteness but do not give him any serious attention." But such a study would also focus on the author, and it would illuminate important characteristics of his texts as well. In a time when new scientific discoveries were unsettling traditional Christian faith and discrediting optimistic views of human nature, Dodgson's troubled imagination invoked a Romantic myth of childhood innocence to construct a timeless fantasy retreat from the growing tide of disillusion. Moreover, the privileged and secure Dodgson consciously wrote the *Alices*, as he says in his prefatory poem to *Through the Looking-Glass,* for an upper-middle-class "child of pure unclouded brow," intending to keep her forever a privileged girl of seven or eight, free of any worldly "breath of bale," everlastingly secure in the secluded garden of her father (the dean of Christ Church College, Oxford) and "the pleasance of [Carroll's] fairy-tale" (*L*, 103).

Finally, some mention should be made of the countless Lewis Carroll spin-offs and their role in sustaining the ever-expanding, worldwide *Alice* institution—the endless parade of consumer goods and advertising gimmicks based on the *Alices*; the hordes of imitative children's books, recordings, films, videotapes, and computer games; the dolls, toys, souvenirs, and physical artifacts of every description; and the daily verbal and pictorial allusions to *Wonderland* and *Looking-Glass* in all areas of modern life and material culture. These too play a part in the critical reception of the *Alices*, for they reinforce the powerful fetishism that has surrounded the books for nearly a century, thus fostering a peculiar reverence among the many readers who approach them as one might approach a sacred text, a text in this case quoted almost as often as the Holy Bible (and alluded to by many worshipers and admirers who have never actually read them). Out of this beatified aura have emerged a number of valuable critical interpretations as well as many first-rate works of art—most recently, for example, Barry Moser's stunning wood-engraving illustrations for the 1982–83 University of California Press editions; David Del Tredici's large body of splendid *Alice* concert pieces composed since 1968; the Czech animated filmmaker Jan Svankmajer's haunting, surrealistic *Alice* (1984); and the 1985 British film *Dream Child,* which uses charming, larger-than-life, Jim Henson puppets to represent familiar *Alice* creatures, and which dramatizes the views of the elderly Alice Liddell Hargreaves reflecting on her girlhood relationship with the grown-up Mr. Dodgson. Besides the innumerable stage representations that have appeared since the first one in 1886, more than 20 film versions of the *Alices* have been produced since 1903 and more than 10 television versions since 1966. All of these spin-offs are, in a sense, also critical readings of Carroll's texts: they constitute verbal, musical, and visual interpretations of the *Alices* that can often enhance our understanding of the books' power and perennial popularity. But time does not permit a discussion of these and many other manifestations of the major cultural institution that began so modestly one July afternoon in 1862 when a shy and unknown Oxford don told his extemporaneous Alice tales to three of his treasured child friends with no thought of where in the world his *Alices* would lead.[7]

A Reading

4

Alice's Adventures in Wonderland: An Underground Journey to the End of Night*

"But I don't want to go among mad people," Alice remarked.
"Oh, you can't help that." said the Cat: "we're all mad here."

When Charles Dodgson developed into a written text the oral, freely associated, extemporaneous Alice stories he first told to the young Liddell sisters (even before he probably had any notion of publishing them), he entitled them *Alice's Adventures under Ground* (1862–63), an elaborate little volume he painstakingly printed by hand and illustrated for Alice Liddell's exclusive ownership. The title of that volume, essentially an abbreviated version of the book we know today as Lewis Carroll's *Alice's Adventures in Wonderland* (1865), makes excellent sense: Alice's adventures do occur literally under the ground; but, more important, like an underground publication or an underground political movement, they constitute an underground response to Alice's ordinary, wide-awake existence, a comically disguised subversion of the above-ground world's accepted, more or less "official" grounds of meaning and order.

Whatever Dodgson's reasons for choosing "under Ground" as the key terms in the title for his first, private version of *Wonderland,* the

*This chapter is based on "Alice's Journey to the End of the Night," *PMLA* 81, no. 5 (October 1966): 313–26.

choice is therefore remarkably appropriate. Perhaps even the final version would be better entitled *Alice's Adventures under Ground,* since, like its original, it represents a surprisingly comprehensive subversive attack upon the commonsense, pragmatic reasonableness that made the bourgeois Victorian's waking life, as it makes our own, manageable and sane. *Alice's Adventures in Wonderland* can thus be understood as, among other things, a comic horror vision of the chaotic land beneath the seemingly "natural," permanent, and sensible groundworks constructed by Western thought and middle-class social convention.

Alice's dogged quest for Wonderland's meaning in terms of her above-ground world of secure assumptions and self-assured regulations is doomed to failure. Her only escape, finally, is in flight from Wonderland's maddening anarchy—a desperate leap back to the above-ground certainty of socia' formalities and ordinary logic. Moreover, Alice's literal quest serves vicariously as her readers' metaphorical search for meaning in the lawless, haphazard universe of their own deepest consciousness. The fact that *Wonderland* is a literary dream vision thus turns out to be far more than a matter of technical classification. If it were merely that, one might dismiss the work as simply a whimsical, dreamy excursion into an amusing, childlike world that bears little relevance to the central concerns of adult life and little importance in comparison to the obviously "serious" texts that explore these concerns. But if "dream vision" is understood as profound thinkers (ranging from medieval poets to modern psychologists) have so often understood it, as an avenue to knowledge that is perhaps more meaningful—and frequently more horrifying—than any that the unaided conscious intellect can discover, then it provides an accurate description of the very substance of *Alice's Adventures in Wonderland.*

Merely to list the reverses Alice encounters underground is to survey at a glance an almost total destruction of the fabric of our self-styled logical, orderly, and coherent approach to the world. Practically all pattern, save the consistency of chaos, is annihilated. First, there are the usual modes of thought—ordinary mathematics and logic: in Wonderland they possess no meaning. Next are the basic social and linguistic conventions: these too lose all validity. Finally, the fundamental frame-work of conscious predication—orderly time and space—appears no-where except in the confused memory of the befuddled but obstinate little visitor from above ground. Alice becomes therefore the reader's surrogate on a frightful journey into meaningless night. The only differ-ence between Alice and the reader—and this is very significant—is that she soberly, tenaciously, childishly refuses to accept chaos completely for what it is, while adult readers almost invariably respond with the only defense left open to them in the face of unquestionable chaos: they laugh. Naturally they laugh for other reasons, too. But the essence of Alice's adventures beneath commonly accepted ground is the grimmest comedy conceivable, the comedy of humankind's absurd condition in an apparently random, meaningless world.

If *Alice's Adventures in Wonderland* is, then, best understood as a grimly comic trip through the lawless underground that lies just beneath the surface of our constructed universe, what gives the work its indisput-able relevance to that universe, what keeps the book itself from becom-ing formless, inconsistent, hopelessly confusing, and deeply troubling? The answers to these questions provide a revelation of the book's liter-ary nature, a probable explanation of its enormous popularity, and a tentative glimpse at a fundamental problem of existence in modern culture.

In the Beginning

Alice begins her subterranean journey simply because she is curious: she follows the White Rabbit down the rabbit hole, "never once consid-ering how in the world she was to get out again" (W, 8). With the fearlessness of the innocent child, the intellectual and spiritual reckless-ness of a heedless scientist or saint, Alice takes her gigantic, apparently irreversible, leap into the world beneath ordinary human experience. Significantly, however, Alice brings along with her a number of things from that old world above ground, the most important being her faith in the simple orderliness of the universe. Thus, in the midst of her long, inexplicable fall she retains her old belief in regular causal relations and puts the empty marmalade jar back into a cupboard in order to avoid "killing somebody underneath," whatever "killing somebody" might have meant in the 1860s to a sheltered, bourgeois English child of seven. She wonders, as she falls and falls, about many things—all in terms of the world she has left behind, as if she had not really left it at all. She wonders, for instance, what latitude or longitude she has arrived at, even though "latitude" and "longitude" are not only meaningless words to her, but also meaningless measurements under the ground. She wonders also whether she will come out on the other side of the earth, where people called "the antipathies" (W, 8) walk with their heads downwards (an unintended but prophetic play on the word *antipodes,* for most of the contrary "people" she will meet down under will be truly "antipathies" to Alice).

Already a pattern is discernible: Alice's assumptions are typically no more than her elders' operating premises, which she maintains with a childish credulity that caricatures doctrinaire and ignorant assuredness or blind faith. For her these premises are frequently empty words and arbitrary signs, yet her belief in their validity is almost absolute. Carroll thus economically establishes one crucial facet of his heroine before her Wonderland adventures and her quest for meaning begin in earnest: she has reached that characteristic developmental stage in which the world and its words appear completely explainable, where all questions have answers, where mysteries and paradoxes are simply puzzles awaiting inevitable solutions. With a few deft touches, Carroll has prepared us for Alice's first major confrontation with chaos. She is ready to cope with the "impossible" in terms of the "possible," and we are ready to understand and laugh at her literal-minded, confident reactions.

To all of us the concept of constant or predictable size is important; to a child of seven it is often a matter of physical and emotional survival. However, since Alice wants desperately to pass through the tiny door into the "loveliest garden you ever saw" (W, 10), she herself wishes the destruction of the cherished principle of constant size: she wishes she could find the way to shut up like a telescope (to grow backwards, so to speak, to an unlost Eden). Fortunately, "so many out-of-the-way things had happened lately" that she has "begun to think that very few things indeed [are] really impossible" (*W*, 10). Here Alice's mind is operating along logical lines established before her arrival in the confusing underground: she deals with the impossible as if it had to conform to the regular causal operations of her old world above ground. But the adult reader is likely to be skeptical: besides recognizing the fallacies of Alice's reasoning in terms of traditional above-ground logic, that reader also understands that in an underground world where "impossibility" is, as it were, the rule, Alice has no basis to assume that the old logic still applies.

In any event, Alice is comparatively successful this time—her apparent logic seems valid. But while her ability to change her size at will is at first pleasurable (as it well might be to children, who often equate size with power), it soon becomes a mixed blessing. Although she "had got so much into the way of expecting nothing but out-of-the-way things to happen, that it seemed quite dull and stupid for life to go on in the common way" (*W*, 13),[1] rapid, almost haphazard changes from 10 inches to 9 feet are accompanied by downright dangerous circumstances like deep pools of tears and frightfully cramped quarters. Nevertheless, even here Wonderland still seems to bear some relationship to above-ground causality: growing big or small appears to have predictable effects. Amid all the comedy, however (and with Alice's unwitting help), the ominous destructive process has begun: two reasonably constant aspects of ordinary existence—natural progressive growth and predictable size—have already lost their apparent validity. And whether or not Alice recognizes it, a big wedge has been driven into her old structure of meaning.

ALICE'S IDENTITY

In these circumstances of growing confusion, Alice naturally tries to relate herself to the secure stability of her past existence. She soon says, "Dear, dear! How queer everything is to-day! And yesterday things went on just as usual. . . . [I]f I'm not the same, the next question is, 'Who in the world am I?' Ah, *that's* the great puzzle!" (*W*, 15–16). This "in-the-world" approach bears watching. Earlier, Alice followed the White Rabbit, "never once considering how *in the world* she was to get out again" (*W*, 8; my italics). She typically persists in fruitless attempts to relate her truly "out-of-the-world" adventures to her previous "in-the-world" assumptions. Hence, perhaps sensing that her above-ground identity rested on arbitrary, constructed systems like arithmetic, she attempts to reestablish that "in-the-world" identity by reciting her rote-learned lessons: "Let me see: four times five is twelve, and four times six is thirteen, and four times seven is—oh dear! I shall never get to twenty at that rate!" (*W*, 16). But Alice is in Wonderland, where old assumptions—that rabbits cannot talk, that long falls result in injuries, that longitude and latitude can always plot position, that size and growth must be fairly regular and progressive—have already proven ridiculously invalid. Of course, her arithmetic (as some specialists have pointed out) still makes sense,[2] but only to a mathematically sophisticated mind; and even then the sense it makes only serves to strengthen the book's unfolding vision of the relative, arbitrary nature of common above-ground approaches to meaning. Alice herself has an early intuition of this truth when she asserts, "However, the Multiplication-Table doesn't signify: let's try Geography" (*W*, 16–17). But even before she begins her confused and illogical geography recitation ("London is the capital of Paris," and so on), the reader suspects that she is again headed for failure, since the ordinary concept of space, too, is in Wonderland already well on its way to oblivion.

Directly after these arithmetical and geographical setbacks, Alice attempts to establish her previous identity by means of another above-ground system of "meaning": by reciting Isaac Watts's conventional moral verses about the busy bee and Satan's mischief for idle hands. Once again it is all wrong. Even her voice sounds "hoarse and strange," as if some uncontrollable thing inside her were taking demonic delight in the gruesome parody ("How doth the little croco-dile").[3] In Alice's recitation of this one short comic poem, another important above-ground principle is effectively subverted. For regardless of the patent sentimentality of verses like "How doth the little busy bee/Improve each shining hour," they are for many young children the only morality they yet know (indeed, the very triteness of such verses reflects a truth about the ostensibly more sincere moral aphorisms of adults). Moreover, Alice's comic recitation denies the sentimental convention that animals (like very young children) are innately innocent, naturally good moral agents. And this subversion fits in neatly with Alice's later encounters with the animals of Wonderland: for the most part they will not be like Watts's busy little bee—they will be more like Alice's nasty Darwinian crocodile.[4] Common moral precepts, like orderly growth, are cruelly twisted or rendered silly and meaningless in Wonderland. And with so many familiar, comforting concepts already lost, Alice naturally begins to sense her frightening isolation, her alienation from the self-defining constructs of aboveground culture. It is not long therefore before she fervently wishes that those conventional people she left above ground would call her back because she is, as she cries aloud, "so *very* tired of being all alone here!" (*W*, 17).

Psychoanalytic interpretations of the *Alices* often stress the importance of their self-identity motif, employing complex, questionable therapeutic theory to demonstrate that Alice's dreams symbolize anxious responses to various threats upon her psychic integrity. Psychoanalytic techniques, however, seem superfluous in this case: most adult readers easily recognize that this crucial above-ground convention, the persistent, nearly universal Western belief in permanent self-identity is put to the test and comically demolished in Wonderland.

Alice is constantly perplexed with the same exasperating question: "Who am I?" When, in the fourth chapter, the White Rabbit orders her about like his housemaid Mary Ann, Alice—attempting as usual to relate her outlandish adventures to some orderly pattern in above-ground experience—accepts the new role and imagines how the new identity will follow her back up to her own homeland where her cat Dinah will also treat her like a servant (*W*, 27). This Wonderland reversal of ordinary domination patterns (which also undermines the ideology of "nature" and "natural" hierarchies frequently invoked in ruling-class discourse as a validation for arbitrary privilege and social class rankings) will continue throughout *Wonderland,* as many of the "lower" creatures order Alice about. Like Alice's continuing changes in size, this reversal represents a variation of Wonderland's pervasive interrogation of stable identity, since changes in power relationships, like changes in size, symbolize profound changes in identity. Alice's tortured "What *will* become of me?" (*W,* 28) in reaction to her apparently uncontrolled growth and her fearful acceptance of the role as servant to a rabbit constitutes, then, more than a Victorian upper-middle-class girl's amusing reactions to general, disorienting confusion: it constitutes her heartfelt reaction to the destruction of several fundamental above-ground assumptions that give coherence to her old world—the concepts of orderly, progressive growth and development; of "natural" hierarchical relations between animals and human beings (as well as between various members of a highly stratified, class-ordered society); and, consequently, of rationally consistent human identity.

Not only is Alice's previous identity apparently meaningless in Wonderland; the very concept of permanent identity is invalid. A pack of cards can also be a group of living people, a child can quickly turn into a pig, a cat's grin can exist without a cat. Even inanimate objects like stones lack simple consistency: in the fourth chapter, when the White Rabbit and his crowd throw pebbles at Alice, who is trapped by her enormous size in the house which is now far too small for her, she notices "with some surprise, that the pebbles [are] all turning into little cakes." Well schooled in the above-ground principles of regular causality and by now quite determined to assume that the same principles are operative in this Wonderland of impossibilities, Alice proceeds in her doggedly logical manner: "If I eat one of these cakes . . . it's sure to make *some* change in my size; and, as it can't possibly make me larger, it must make me smaller, I suppose" (*W,* 32). Alice's "I suppose" here humorously hints at what is happening somewhere inside her. Pedestrian as her mind might ordinarily be, she is beginning to get a glimmer of the "principle" of Wonderland—that it operates on *no* recognizable principle whatsoever. Yet her subsequent eating of the pebbles that are now little cakes represents her stubborn determination to act as if her above-ground system of syllogistic order still obtains.

LANGUAGE UPENDED

From the very beginning of the adventures, another common above-ground convention—that verbal communication is potentially logical and unambiguous—has been surreptitiously assailed. Finally, when Alice and the strange animals emerge soaking from the literal pool of her tears, linguistic order dissolves completely—appropriately in the form of dramatized, literalized puns. The Mouse announces in all seriousness that he will dry them; his method is to recite a passage from a history textbook, the "driest thing" he knows (*W*, 22). Here Wonderland, through the comic agency of the actual, wet pool of tears and the Mourse's "dry" history lesson, subverts a fundamental principle of everyday language. These confusions of symbol and object, of metaphorical and literal language, of verbal sign and thing signified, have far-reaching metaphysical significance; but at their simplest, most dramatic level, the confusions contribute one more important component to the pattern of disintegration that pervades Alice's underground adventures.

Much of the humor in this chapter, which centers on the semantic mix-up over the word *dry,* is based on similar linguistic mayhem. The assembled creatures cannot accept language on its own grounds. They want it to do what it cannot do. For one thing, they want it to be consistently logical and self-sufficient. When the Mouse states in his "dry" tale that Stigland "found it advisable," he is interrupted by the Duck, who wants to know the antecedent noun for "it" before the Mouse has a chance to continue (*W*, 22). Here is a twist in Wonderland's destructive strategy: instead of contradicting the validity of human constructs and conventions by simply carrying on without them, Wonderland this time manages in the very act of using them to be far more subversive. Actually, the Duck's demand represents a dramatic reductio ad absurdum of traditional grammar. He implicitly puts above-ground linguistic assumptions to the test by asking language to do what is finally impossible: to be constantly unambiguous, to pull itself up independently by its own very fallible bootstraps. Such a new turn in strategy enriches the complexity of Wonderland's humorous attack on above-ground convention and the illusion of cosmic order. By demanding that language be consistently sequential, Wonderland, so to speak, destroys the meretricious logic of language with logic itself. This new strategy demonstrates one more weapon in Wonderland's comic arsenal: when the world above ground claims to be strictly consistent—as in space, size, or mathematics, for example—Wonderland is, by its very operations, maddeningly inconsistent. But when the world above ground is admittedly inconsistent—as in traditional English grammar and syntax—then Wonderland strenuously demands complete consistency. Such an oblique attack forces adult readers to remember what they always knew: one cannot expect ordinary language to be unambiguous and internally consistent like ordinary mathematics. However, the urgent, rude insistence of Wonderland creatures (like the Eaglet's cry "Speak English!" [W, 22] or later the March Hare's "say what you mean" [W, 55] with its implication that language is not logically reversible like mathematical equations) neatly satirizes the common world's absurd illogicality; and so, in the midst of all the fun, one more conventional prop of above-ground order begins to crumble.

As chapter 3 progresses, this conventional prop finally disintegrates. When Alice asks the Dodo what a "Caucus-Race" is (that is, when she asks him to define a word with other words) and thereby puts to the test a fundamental working principle of language, his only answer is "the best way to explain it is to do it" (W, 23). When the Mouse asserts that his "is a long and a sad tale," Alice replies, "It is a long tail . . . but why do you call it sad?" When the Mouse says "not," Alice thinks he refers to a knot (W, 24–26). Here, then, another above-ground assumption (and one that perplexed Dodgson all his life)—that ordinary language, whether written or spoken, has at least the potential to be univocal and self-sufficient—dissolves as swiftly and easily as the smiling Cheshire Cat. As Alice's adventures continue, this comic subversion of linguistic conventions increases in both scope and intensity.

Chapter 3 foreshadows another feature of linguistic confusion that will reach its absurd apex in the hilarious final pages of the book. The Mouse's tale, printed emblematically in the shape of a mouse's long tail, is about the law. And ordinary conceptions of the law depend in great measure on the common assumption that language, at the bottom of most legal systems, is potentially unambiguous. The word *trial* itself ideally connotes a suspension of judgment as well as a final decision. But in the Mouse's tail/tale, as in the final trial of *Wonderland* (and in may violently distorted trials represented in expressionistic fiction since 1865),[5] the prosecutor can also be the judge and jury, and a judgment can be passed before the trial has begun.

THE CATERPILLAR'S RUDENESS

In chapter 5, "Advice from a Caterpillar," the destruction of the above-ground hierarchy of animals and humans steps up in intensity. This chapter also continues to develop the book's consistent assault on Alice's faith in orderly language, relating that faith to another set of worldly conventions, the customs of social etiquette. The Caterpillar plays a role similar to Humpty Dumpty's in *Through the Looking-Glass:* although he is by no means the incisive, dominating critic of language that Humpty Dumpty is, he is just as rude in his disparagement of Alice's linguistic habits, demonstrating by his actions that the above-ground conventions of etiquette in social intercourse are meaningless in Wonderland. Alice has already suffered the rudeness of the White Rabbit, but the brusque orders of that timid authoritarian seem almost polite in comparison to the outright, boorish hostility of the assertive Caterpillar. Significantly, Alice's own politeness to the Caterpillar increases in inverse proportion to his mounting rudeness: as his demands upon her patience reach fantastic heights of coarseness, she makes it a point to address him as "Sir" and to reply "very politely" to his ludicrously unfair criticisms of her speech, "swallowing down her anger as well as she [can]" (*W*, 35–36). Such diplomatic reactions from Alice, occurring as they do in many places in the *Alices*, are further evidence of her general attempt to find (or impose) an order underground or behind the looking-glass that somehow corresponds to the order of her previous life. Certainly, in that life it is sometimes the most impolite, imperious people who command the most respect and obedience; and to a young child under the domination of inscrutable adults such a paradox may seem orderly and proper.

The Caterpillar's most impolite remark is his very first sentence— the laconic, contemptuous "Who are *you*?" With characteristic comic understatement, the narrator quietly observes in a dramatic aside that "this was not an encouraging opening for a conversation" (*W*, 35). Indeed, in the light of Alice's previous chaotic physical changes and her resultant anxieties about self-identity, the Caterpillar's direct, unvarnished question (like the even ruder variation the Pigeon asks Alice later in the chapter, "*What* are you?" [*W*, 43]) is much more hostile than an ordinary impolite remark: its threatening metaphysical implications greatly intensify its plain rudeness, turning a common social transaction into an ominous existential catechism.

Alice's shaky answer—"I—I hardly know, Sir"—expresses her anxious awareness of the question's far-reaching threats to her once sure, but rapidly deteriorating sense of self. The Caterpillar responds, insisting, "Explain yourself!" Her choice of words hints at the sources of her anxiety: "I can't explain *myself*, I'm afraid, Sir . . . because I'm not myself, you see" (*W*, 35). If selfhood is, as many have argued, not an inherent attribute of each individual but a cultural construct contingent upon various discourses external and prior to the existence of that individual, if the human concept of self is no more than an artifact that derives from external cultural forces, then Alice's remarks here could be read as a sign of her growing awareness that she (her self) is completely contingent on the discursive world in which she finds herself. Thus far, as I have shown, she has instinctually attempted to ground her identity in the terms of her old above-ground world. Now in this brief conversation with the Caterpillar, she appears to be reaching a consciousness that such methods of establishing identity are *from the beginning* futile. As she says here to the Caterpillar, "I can't understand it myself, to begin with." Thus, Alice's earlier "Who in the world am I?" is rapidly revealing itself as a literal, rather than merely a metaphorical "great puzzle" (*W*, 15–16). Indeed, given Wonderland's revelations of the contingent nature of self and world, it is so great a puzzle that it apparently must remain insoluble.

In spite of this growing awareness, however, Alice soon makes another brave attempt to ground herself in Wonderland by reciting one more rote-learned, moralistic poem from her past. This time she recites in response to the Caterpillar's gruff commands, but the result is the same: once again it comes out all wrong. "You are old, Father William," the lively, subversive parody of Robert Southey's didactic verses, is, like Alice's earlier "How doth the little crocodile," more than a humorous poem. In this chapter's context of outlandish impoliteness, Alice's recitation represents a versified paraphrase of the almost immoral rudeness of the Caterpillar. Alice's Father William is the antithesis of Southey's pious, temperate old man who has come gently to the end of his days. Her Father William has the air of an impolite, indeed violent old rake—and a conniving, commercialistic one at that: " 'In my youth,' said the sage, as he shook his grey locks, / 'I kept all my limbs very supple / By the use of this ointment—one shilling the box— / Allow me to sell you a couple?' " (*W*, 38). The Caterpillar is closer to the truth than Alice is when he tells her that her recitation is not wrong merely because, as she says, "some of the words have got altered"; it is, he asserts, "wrong from beginning to end" (*W*, 41) because it runs counter to the whole moral purpose that governs the original Southey poem. Again in a recitation, Alice has yielded to that uncontrollable imp within her and joined more or less willingly in Wonderland's comic dismantling of orderly above-ground convention.

The rudeness of the Caterpillar also contributes to the continuing, growing antipathy between Alice and the creatures of Wonderland. Generally, she is met in these adventures with condescension or mistrust; and most of the underground creatures she encounters are quick to contradict her, undermining at every opportunity the premises of her trust in the secure grounds of her existence. No doubt there is an element of fear in their authoritarian and destructive rudeness: they probably suspect that Alice, like an adult with children, holds the power of life and death over them. She can deny and reject them completely; she can, apparently, destroy them with a few powerful words like "Nonsense" or "You're nothing but a pack of cards!" But whatever their motives, these creatures of Wonderland are, according to all of Alice's acquired standards of social decorum, extremely discourteous (in fact, since they are strangers and Alice is something like a guest, they should, according to those standards, be more polite, not less). Alice, clinging to her above-ground code of behavior, is either assiduously polite or ignorantly determined to educate them in her old etiquette. Significantly, most of her rules consist of "don'ts," obviously laid down by adults and now taken on complete faith by this literal-minded and rather priggish seven-year-old representative of her culture. At the Mad Tea-Party, for example, Alice says to the Mad Hatter, "You should learn not to make personal remarks . . . it's very rude" (W, 55). But here again, as in Wonderland's attacks on her illogical language, Alice's conventions are wittily turned upon themselves: when she violates her own dogmatic principle of decorum and rudely says to the Hatter, "Nobody asked *your* opinion," he "triumphantly" retorts, "Who's making personal remarks now?" (W, 59). And poor Alice finds herself at a new impasse: she does "not quite know what to say to this" (W, 59). She has, without consciously willing it, joined in the pervasive rude spirit of Wonderland; she has been tested by her own principles and has been discredited, putting her, significantly, at a loss for *words*.

In the same Caterpillar episode, the narrative touches so lightly upon another absurd "impossibility" that it is likely to escape a reader's attention the way it completely escapes Alice's. The Caterpillar leaves Alice with a rudeness so blatant and shocking that it is funny: he "yawned once or twice . . . got down off the mushroom, and crawled away into the grass, merely remarking, as [he] went, 'One side will make you grow taller, and the other side will make you grow shorter.' " In a quandary, Alice thinks to herself, "One side of *what*? The other side of *what*?" And the Caterpillar says, " 'Of the mushroom,' . . . just as if she had asked it aloud" (*W*, 41). No more is said about this amazing occurrence, but readers may well be impressed by such clairvoyance. For it is still one of our cherished above-ground beliefs that communication between separate minds necessitates some exchange of tangible signs; and even if we admit the validity of extrasensory phenomena, we do so with some wonder and uneasiness. But the Caterpillar accepts his clairvoyance as a matter of course: there is not the slightest trace of wonder, curiosity, or fear in his nonchalant attitude. The fact that Alice fails to notice the Caterpillar's astonishing mental feat—fails, that is, to relate this extraordinary incident to her pre-Wonderland experience—is in part explained by the nonchalance of the Caterpillar. But her failure might also be taken as a measure of her assimilation into Wonderland's chaos: she seems to be losing sight of her old standards of reference, drifting dangerously toward an unwilled acceptance of Wonderland's persistent violations of the laws and conventions of her old world. Experiencing so many subversive wonders in such rapid succession seems to be taking its toll, threatening the loss of Alice's precious sense of innocent wonder and curiosity as well as her sense of rational order. On the other hand, she also seems at this point to have begun—in a tentative and unconscious fashion—to draw back a little, to withhold her wonder, sensing that Wonderland endangers the integrity of her old identity because it in no way corresponds to her former world above ground, even though she will in later adventures still persist in her attempts to find or construct a meaningful correspondence.

The creatures in chapter 6, like the complacently clairvoyant Caterpillar, consider their environment and their actions normal: to them there is certainly nothing particularly curious or wonderful about Wonderland. This crucial aspect of Wonderland's chaos is made explicit when a large plate comes skimming out the door, barely missing the Frog-Footman's head, and the narrator reports that the footman continues what he is doing, "exactly as if nothing had happened" (*W*, 46). This easy acceptance of chaos by the inhabitants of Wonderland bears at least two significant relations to the book's major concerns. First, it serves to pique further Alice's curiosity about the "rules" of Wonderland. Since the creatures clearly do not think their lives and world are in any way strange or disorderly, Alice takes this attitude—albeit incorrectly—as a sign that there must be be an order, an order that she does not yet comprehend. In general, she fails to consider consciously the possibility that the anarchy of their realm may be directly related to their own heedless and irrational behavior—that they live in chaos and thus act accordingly. Indeed, her reason, ordering mechanism that it is, is totally incapable of functioning outside the bounds of some system of order. Second, the creatures' acceptance of chaos can be viewed as a fantastic satire of what happens every day in Alice's world above ground. Here in fact may be the correlation between the two worlds that Alice seeks but never fully discovers. The human creatures above ground, with their innumerable constructs and arbitrary conventions, act in essentially the same way. If Wonderland's Frog-Footman, say, were to visit the London of the 1860s, would not the average Englishman's complacent acceptance of such preposterous notions as orderly, consistent time and space strike the Frog-Footman as insane? This gently comic exposure of the relativity of order is an important component of *Wonderland*'s vision of universal anarchy, for what humankind (or Alice in her subterranean adventures) typically desires is *not* an adjustable, fluid, and contingent frame of meaning, but an unambiguous, sure, and permanent order. Alice's fervent reaction to the Frog-Footman's argumentativeness perhaps signifies her growing general reaction to this universal anarchy: "It's really dreadful . . . the way all the creatures argue. It's enough to drive one crazy!" (*W*, 46). Like her previous "I suppose" (*W*, 32), the key words, the trite but accurate "dreadful" and "crazy," subtly reveal what is happening to Alice without her knowing it: she is slowly coming to a full perception of Wonderland's maddening—and dreadfully dangerous—nature.

THE DUCHESS'S CRUELTY

Soon Alice meets the Duchess whose hilarious rudeness surpasses even the Caterpillar's. Alice again responds with her best above-ground manners. The Duchess, like the Frog-Footman, takes no notice of the bedlam around her: surrounded by the howling of the baby, the hail of kitchen utensils thrown by the cook, and the general domestic disorder, she single-mindedly persists in her barbarous treatment of the baby and her guest Alice. Her "lullaby" is another of Wonderland's subversive verse parodies. For example, a stanza of the original poem by David Bates reads,

> Speak gently to the little child!
> Its love be sure to gain;
> Teach it in accents soft and mild—
> It may not long remain.

The Duchess sings,

> Speak roughly to your little boy,
> And beat him when he sneezes:
> He only does it to annoy,
> Because he knows it teases.
> (*W*, 48)

This parody, like the earlier ones uttered by Alice, implicitly controverts Alice's previous, above-ground moral code. The Duchess, so fond of aphorisms ("Everything's got a moral, if only you can find it" [*W*, 70]), here recommends what Alice's world would call sheer cruelty. Moreover, the Duchess practices what she preaches, constantly shaking and tossing the baby as she sings her "lullaby."

In a dramatized representation of the dreadful threats that Darwin's recently enunciated theory posed for precious bourgeois notions of self-esteem and "natural" dominance (*The Origin of Species* was published only three years before Dodgson began to expand his *under Ground* stories into *Wonderland*), the Duchess's baby suddenly devolves into an ugly, grunting pig—right in Alice's hands! This spectacular regressive event instantaneously and graphically undermines the foolish, initial Victorian accommodation with the theory of evolution as inherently progressive. Surreptitiously but firmly, it gives the comic lie to widely held convictions, like the one that concludes Tennyson's extremely popular *In Memoriam* (1850), that humankind stands at the growing tip of nature, passing "thro' life of lower phase," "no longer half-akin to brute" (section 131, lines 125, 133), "the roof and crown of things" ("The Lotos-Eaters," 1842, line 69).

The brief pig-baby episode and the accompanying Tenniel illustration also constitute a graphic denial of the conventional sentimental attitude toward children (the Duchess even shouts "Pig!" at the baby), another Wonderland send-up of above-ground sentiment and morality. It is worth noting here that Dodgson himself, usually so fearful of committing any social impropriety, could not in his letters and conversation always restrain his deep-seated disgust with babies, despite his adoration of little girls. But such information merely corroborates what the adult reader easily perceives: the pig-baby episode humorously dramatizes the arbitrary nature of conventional attitudes toward infants as well as toward the inherent dignity of all human beings, children or adults. One need go no further than the text—Alice herself muses about "other children she knew, who might do very well as pigs" (W, 50).

A CAT'S ADVICE

In this same chapter Alice has her famous conversation with the Cheshire Cat. In view of Wonderland's mounting subversion of the common world's principal foundations for sanity and order, the Cat's remarks become especially important. He is the one Wonderland creature who explicitly presents Alice with a broad-based, ostensibly reasonable explanation of the chaos that surrounds her. When Alice asserts, "I don't want to go among mad people," the Cat replies, "Oh, you can't help that. . . . [W]e're all made here. I'm mad. You're mad." Alice answers, "How do you know I am mad?" And the Cat says, "You must be or you wouldn't have come here" (W, 51). Through this brief exchange, the amused reader—not Alice—gets a tentative, fleeting glimpse at the fundamental meaning of Wonderland that Alice instinctively seeks.

Furthermore, the enigmatic Cat, who vanishes and appears as easily as he smiles, here intimates that Alice's curiosity is madness or at least the motive behind her mad act, her heedless leap into this incorrigibly insane underground. That Alice is, as the Cat states, just as mad as the natives of Wonderland is still difficult for most readers to admit, even to perceive. For Alice comes from and alone represents the everyday world of her readers, which, for the sake of their existence as well as hers, must appear sane. The narrator blandly asserts, "Alice didn't think that [his syllogism] proved it [her madness] at all" (W, 51), and the reader laughs and tacitly agrees, forgetting that the Cat's reasoning can be just as valid as Alice's. For Alice, like the Cheshire Cat, is now deep underground in Wonderland.

Alice apparently learns nothing from the Cat's important revelation. While she is "not much surprised" at his vanishing, for she is "getting so well used to queer things happening" (W, 52), she still fails to perceive Wonderland's meaning for those who live by the illusory principles of above-ground order. Furthermore, after being told specifically by the Cheshire Cat that the Hatter and the March Hare are both mad, Alice, when she meets them in her next adventure, remains uninstructed and stubbornly persists in her futile attempts to relate their crazy, disordered actions to her old notions of order and sanity.

Is it because Alice is a child that she fails after all this to see the mad Wonderland for what it is? Is it her youthful ignorance or her insatiable curiosity that makes her miss the perilous significance of a grin without a cat? All she can think at this point is, "Well! I've often seen a cat without a grin, but a grin without a cat! It's the most curious thing I ever saw in all my life!" (W, 53). But Alice's reaction here represents the response of most adults, too. In a sense, all of us are often childishly ignorant in the face of supreme danger, for woven into the complex fabric of implications in this laughable colloquy with the Cat is one implication that easily escapes even our attention: the very principle of predication by which we know—the seemingly indestructible bond between subject and attribute, a crucial element in the logic by which we live our rational lives—has been graphically subverted by the laughable appearance of a cat's grin without a cat.

THE END OF TIME

In chapter 7 Alice's former concept of time dissolves, in one of the funniest and yet most grimly destructive scenes in the book. While many other common grounds for order continue to be subverted in this adventure, "A Mad Tea-Party" focuses on time, one major above-ground system of order that still appears to have some validity. For up to this point, the attack on time has been only incidental and certainly not overwhelming, and time still has had some apparent validity if only because the narrative itself has progressed through a vaguely chronological framework.

In the beginning of "A Mad Tea-Party," however, Alice comes upon a situation that apparently has had no temporal beginning and probably will never have an end. The March Hare, Mad Hatter, and Dormouse sit at a tea table, engaged in a truly endless succession of tea and pointless, disjointed conversation (perhaps a fantastic representation of a young child's view of polite mealtimes). In the midst of all the disconnected talk, the Hatter suddenly asks Alice, as if it were a test, "What day of the month is it?" and, like the White Rabbit, looks at his watch "uneasily" (W, 55).[6] This question opens a series of ridiculous comments on watches and time. These comments themselves seem pointless, and their apparent lack of coherence or sequence intensifies the chapter's pervasive atmosphere of timelessness (especially since Alice, like the ordinary nineteenth-century reader, still clings to her old conception of time—and narrative—as linear and progressive).

When the Hatter admits that his ostensibly pregnant riddle about the raven and the writing desk (like the riddle, for Alice, of the "meaning" of Wonderland itself) has no answer, Alice sighs, "I think you might do something better with the time . . . than wasting it in asking riddles that have no answers." The Hatter replies, "If you knew Time as well as I do . . . you wouldn't talk about wasting it. It's *him*" (W, 56). This nonsensical personification of time continues in the conversation that follows. Amid the by now familiar punning that tends to destroy linguistic order like the punning here on beating or killing time, time, like a person, is characterized as malleable, recalcitrant, or disorderly.

This view of time as finite and personal, of course, comically subverts the above-ground convention of time's infinite, orderly, impersonal, and autonomous nature. This finally puts time in its proper place as another arbitrary, relative, and changeable fiction that has no claim to absolute validity, no binding claim, in fact, to existence. Since time is now like a person, a kind of ill-behaved child created by human beings, there is the unavoidable danger that he will rebel and refuse to act consistently. That is exactly what has happened in the Wonderland tea party: the Hatter says time "won't do a thing I ask! It's always six o'clock now" (*W*, 58), that is, it is always teatime. Time is thus frozen in timelessness,[7] and one of the most important concepts underlying common human experience is laughed out of existence.

Wonderland seems to compensate for frozen time by substituting space: the creatures move around the tea table in a kind of never-ending game of musical chairs. We might take this substitution of space as Carroll's hint at a more accurate, more "scientific" conception of time; but, like the underlying accuracy of Alice's confused multiplication tables in chapter 2, this subtle hint at the reality of "reality" is probably too sophisticated for many readers, as it certainly is for poor Alice. Besides, the concept of space, as we have seen, has already been thoroughly demolished. At this midway point in the narrative, then, the destruction of the foundations of Alice's old order is practically complete.

Thus, by chapter 7 (the center of the 12-chapter, mock-epic underworld journey) Alice has reached almost rock bottom in her descent into chaos—betokened by the word *mad*, which is part of the title of the chapter, part of the name of one principal character, and part of the common epithet applied to another ("mad as a March Hare"). Her dramatic experience of the disintegration of the above-ground system of meaning now seems complete, but at least one groundwork of that old system remains intact: despite the fact that inanimate objects like stones have lost stable identity, they have up to chapter 8 remained within the class of inanimate objects—with the possible exception hinted at in chapter 7 that tea trays can fly like bats. "Twinkle, twinkle, little bat" (*W*, 57), Carroll's enchanting parody of Jane Taylor's nursery rhyme

"The Star," occupies a pivotal position in the pattern of destruction being traced in this chapter. First, the poem uses, as parodies generally do, the familiar original verses as part of the total context.[8] Carroll's substitutions (*bat* for *star, at* for *are, you fly* for *so high,* and *tea tray* for *diamond*) must be considered in the light of Taylor's poem. Viewed this way, Carroll's poem becomes a compressed statement of much of the destruction that has already taken place in Wonderland, as well as a gentle hint at what is to come in the next chapter. A bat represents to most readers ugly violent nature—active, changing and predatory; a star, on the other hand, usually connotes beautiful, remote, unthreatening, and static nature. Moreover, "what you're at" and "fly" intensify the Darwinian, predatory image of gross struggle and increase the humorous incongruity between Carroll's lines and Taylor's. All this harks back to the earlier comic subversion of the sentimental view of animal morality satirized in such verses as "How doth the little crocodile," another send-up of false piety and false natural history in popular nursery rhymes. This, in turn, leads the reader's mind back to the original star, whose moral connotations have now been subverted: it no longer seems to deserve the attribution of unchanging purity implied by "diamond." In addition, 'Twinkle, twinkle, little bat," with its delightful mix-up of animate bat with inanimate star and flying tea tray with flying bat, serves as an appropriate transition to chapter 8 where the constructed separation between animate and inanimate objects is finally destroyed utterly.

THE QUEEN OF HEARTS

Immediately after the highly subversive Mad Tea-Party, Alice meets in chapter 8 a whole new set of creatures—playing cards that are alive, so alive, in fact, that one has become one of the most well-known "persons" in English literature, the ever-furious Queen of Hearts. Carroll's method of making these cards seem human is an example of his technical ability throughout *Wonderland.* For one thing, he skillfully employs devices that make their conversations with Alice appear natu-

ral and ordinary. Almost immediately, for example, one of the garden-
ers, the two of spades, speaks in a slight dialect (dialects have been
used previously for a number of Wonderland creatures, notably for
Pat, the Irish gardener of chapter 4). Carroll also carefully indicates the
volume and emotional tones of the dialogue—a kind of pointed humorous reversal of the persistent above-ground notion that speech is a
primary distinction between animals and humans. Some card characters merely "say" their lines, others "shout" or "roar"; some are
"silent," or speak in "a low, hurried tone"; Alice herself gives "a little
scream of laughter," and the Queen sometimes speaks "in a voice of
thunder" (*W*, 62–68). Another device for making these inanimate
objects appear human and their scenes realistic is the inclusion of
already well-established characters from earlier adventures, characters
like the White Rabbit and the Duchess whose "humanness" is now
taken for granted and who here respond to the playing-card Queen as
if she too were human and supremely vital.

In this way the by now shaky above-ground premise that there is a
distinct cleavage between the animate and inanimate worlds is finally,
humorously overthrown. One thing, however, remains constant: these
card creatures are just as ornery, just as irrational and chaotic as the
other Wonderland inhabitants Alice has already encountered. The
chaos is in fact compounded when these inanimate-objects-turned-
human treat the normally live creatures of Alice's former existence as
inanimate artifacts. Wonderland has again turned the tables, here by
using live animals like hedgehogs and flamingoes for croquet balls and
mallets. Alice, still clinging to her "in-the-world" approach, says to the
Cheshire Cat, "you've no idea how confusing it is all the things being
alive" (*W*, 67). The Cat, of course, has no idea how confusing it is
because he neither possesses nor is possessed by Alice's old, above-
ground standards of regularity. Furthermore, this appeal to the Cat
marks another step in Alice's slowly disintegrating sense of order:
although she still clings to her old concepts of reality, she forgets
completely what the Cat has told her about madness, about what he is
and where he dwells.

Since Alice rarely relinquishes her grounding notions of order without some struggle, it is fitting that in "The Queen's Croquet-Ground" she should try to remind herself of the above-ground distinction between live and inanimate entities. When the Queen of Hearts rudely demands, as so many other creatures have rudely demanded, that Alice identify herself, Alice "very politely" says, "My name is Alice, so please your Majesty," but adds to herself, "Why, they're only a pack of cards, after all. I needn't be afraid of them!" (*W*, 63). At this point, Alice is not yet prepared to say such a subversive thing aloud. Nevertheless, her silent comment to herself here suggests that Alice is beginning to sense the final danger inherent in Wonderland—her own destruction—and is falling back on her only defense against this ultimate devastation, which has lurked ominously beneath all the rest of her problems. She is falling back on those now-inoperative above-ground principles that, illusory or not, can preserve her sanity and her very existence. She is beginning to fight Wonderland's subversiveness with her own.

Alice has many reasons for such defiant thoughts. She has certainly been cheated: the Queen's croquet ground—with its painted flowers, its exasperating, ruleless, demented game, its wild and dangerous creatures—is that same "beautiful garden" she has been seeking from the outset. Perhaps it is the realization that her arduous journey beneath the grounds of her old, dull, constricted world of rote lessons and unexplainable, arbitrary adult rules has brought her, not to those Edenic "beds of bright flowers and those cool fountains" (*W*, 10), but to a chaotic place of madness ruled by a furious Queen who insanely orders pointless executions with almost every breath—perhaps it is the realization of all this that encourages Alice to begin her rebellion.

A more important reason for Alice's drift toward rebellion is that she has come to sense that her quest for unambiguous meaning and immortal order is fruitless. Haphazard as her trip may at first seem, Alice has nevertheless been progressing toward the grounds of Wonderland that correspond to the grounds of her old world. The rulers of Wonderland (the King and Queen of Hearts) and their "beautiful garden" have been Alice's spiritual goal almost from the beginning, and it is appropriate that the rulers and court of Wonderland should hold the secret of their realm's meaning and be the ultimate source of its (putative) rules and order. The fact that they are court cards and hearts emphasizes their central, vital, commanding position, as does the fact that they are introduced with names written all in capital letters, a device stressed by Carroll in his revisions. Ironically, then, Alice is for once correct in judging Wonderland on the basis of her previous "in-the-world" experience. But what do these repositories of meaning and order turn out to be? Mere abstract, manufactured, arbitrary symbols—just a pack of cards: stylized pictures of kings and queens, men and women. Their grounds of meaning turn out to be croquet grounds and their principles, the mad "rules" of an insane, topsy-turvy *game*.

Alice's first realization that she need not be afraid because, "after all," she is dealing with a mere pack of cards has an effect, although an impermanent one, on her subsequent behavior. Immediately after her brief insight, she is extremely rude to the Queen, so rude that Alice herself is "surprised at her own courage." She interrupts the Queen's repeated "Off with her head!" by saying " 'Nonsense!' very loudly and decidedly." The King's and Queen's immediate reactions to this single word are noteworthy: the "Queen was silent" and "the King laid his hand upon her arm and timidly said, 'Consider, my dear: she is only a child!' " (W, 64). Among other things, this reaction of the rulers of Wonderland is a humorous, metaphorical equivalent of the aboveground world's reaction to the ridiculous challenge of a child's Wonderland dream. When either world is named for what it is, it is left, as it were, speechless. Paradoxically, by the power of one of the most artificial constructs of all—the word—these rulers are rendered powerless, that is, without words. That the child Alice has had this supreme power all along goes without saying. Alice, however, does not realize the potency of her weapon or, for that matter, that she even possesses a weapon. Hence, even though she can say to herself that "they're only a pack of cards, after all. I needn't be afraid of them!" she soon reverts to her now seemingly unwarranted fear: "Alice began to feel very uneasy: to be sure, she had not as yet had any dispute with the Queen, but she knew that it might happen any minute, 'and then,' thought she, 'what would become of me? They're dreadfully fond of beheading people here: the great wonder is, that there's any one left alive!' " (*W*, 67).

ALICE'S REBELLION

From this point to the end of the adventures, it is the main business of the narrative to trace Alice's preparation for her final, overt denial of Wonderland, the destruction of her fearful vision for the sake of her identity and sanity. To gain strength and courage for that act of denial, Alice seeks the aid of allies (meanwhile, of course, she continues to play what she has already realized is a crazy game). In chapter 8 she makes the mistake of assuming that the Cheshire Cat is such an ally. She spies his grin in the air and says, "It's the Cheshire Cat: now I shall have somebody to talk to." But when Alice, "feeling very glad she had some one to listen to her," complains to the Cat about the game she is playing—saying "they don't seem to have any rules in particular"— his only reply is the apparent non sequitur, "How do you like the Queen?" (*W*, 67). He, of course, sees no fault in a game without any rules but a mad queen's mad acts.

In much the same way that she mistakes the Cheshire Cat for an ally, Alice mistakenly assumes that "logical" rules still have validity. At the very beginning of the next chapter ("The Mock Turtle's Story"), she meets the Duchess again, and, finding that previously irascible creature in good humor, assumes that her anger was merely the result of the pepper in her soup. "Maybe it's always pepper that makes people hot-tempered," Alice muses. And she begins to extrapolate from her newfound hypothesis, "very much pleased at having found out a new kind of rule" (*W*, 70). Here, despite the prominent "maybe," Alice reveals that she still stubbornly believes there is a reliable cause and effect order in Wonderland and one that can be applied to her own world too—this in spite of all the mounting evidence to the contrary. Indeed, the Duchess herself is the personified reductio ad absurdum of Alice's attitude toward rules: the Duchess finds a "moral" (or rule) in *everything.* Alice is faced with a new curious problem: once again Wonderland forces her above-ground assumptions to the final test, and once again it laughs them out of existence. Poor dogged Alice, however, is unable to see the "moral" in the Duchess's silly preoccupation with finding morals: she fails to perceive that such fatuous remarks as "Everything's got a moral, if only you can find it" (*W,* 70) are essentially satirical counterthrusts at her own dogged, futile determination to find the rules in a ruleless Wonderland.

Finally, however, Alice meets two creatures who seem capable of serving as allies—the chimerical Gryphon and Mock Turtle, two of the most fantastic characters in Wonderland's entire laughable gallery. Both creatures, nonsensical as they are, seem to see Wonderland for what it is—at least for what it is to Alice. When Alice recounts to them her adventures, the Gryphon says, "It's all about as curious as it can be" (*W,* 82). When Alice attempts to recite another moralistic Watts poem (" 'Tis the voice of the sluggard") and again uncontrollably twists it into a cruel, amoral, survival-of-the-fittest commentary on nature, the Mock Turtle asserts that "it sounds uncommon nonsense" and says, "It's by far the most confusing thing I ever heard!" (*W,* 82– 84). Their words "curious," "nonsense," and "confusing" are drawn of course from the most frequently used words in Alice's vocabulary, indicating, perhaps, that these figures are dream projections of what might be called (ironically) Alice's "reality principle" in opposition to her by now discredited, dangerous "fantasy principle." The fact that the two creatures, openly marked by their names and identities as fictive constructs, use Alice's favorite terms to describe Wonderland compounds the linguistic confusion, making a final, complete mockery of Alice's above-ground assumptions about the validity of language.

The sympathy of these creatures for Alice is therefore not as simple as it first appears. Indeed, their solicitude is undoubtedly false. For both creatures are palpable sentimentalists; the Mock Turtle's mawkish song about "beautiful" soup, sung in "a voice choked with sobs" (*W,* 84), provides the measure of their sentimentality. Once again Wonderland tests an above-ground convention by carrying it to its extreme: here, instead of attacking one particular kind of above-ground sentiment such as the common emotional response to babies or to stars and bees, Wonderland comically overthrows sentiment itself. Alice cannot hope to find genuine sympathy and real allies in the Gryphon and Mock Turtle. In any event she has no time to react, for the great trial of the last chapters is about to begin.

Before turning to that trial, however, we should try to assess the general function of the Mock Turtle and Gryphon in the Wonderland motif of subversion I have traced in this chapter. After the Queen's croquet game, no remnant of ordinary above-ground order remains intact. The only order poor Alice can possibly perceive in Wonderland is the consistent antipathy of all the creatures toward her and all her previous assumptions. Now, chapters 9 and 10 seem to subvert and finally destroy the "order" of Wonderland itself, because here the two sentimental friends, the Gryphon and the Mock Turtle, argue neither with each other (as do most of the other creatures) nor with Alice's above-ground assumptions. This sympathy—whether genuine or false—breaks Wonderland's pattern of antipathy and is perhaps the ultimate destruction: order as Alice once knew it is now so hopelessly snarled that she must, in literal self-defense, leap back to her own insane, illusory, but livable above-ground world of arbitrary, constructed logic and convention.[9]

If "The Queen's Croquet-Ground" has convinced Alice that her quest for Wonderland's principle of order in the personalities or games of Wonderland's playing-card rulers is pointless, the last two chapters of the book reveal that even beyond these rulers and their mad croquet ground there is no fundamental law, save perhaps the furious Queen's "Off with his head!" and even that persistent demand, Alice has been told by the Gryphon, is never obeyed ("It's all her fancy, that: they never executes nobody, you know" [W, 74]).

At the end, Alice is finally brought to what should be the last refuge, the ultimate grounds of order—the court of law. Chapter 11 begins with a crowd scene. As the chapter progresses, we realize that many of the creatures Alice has encountered from the beginning are assembled here. This strengthens the impression that the trial is the final, public test of Wonderland's meaning, the appropriate conclusion of Alice's quest for law and order. What is on trial here is not really the Knave of Hearts. What is on trial is the "law" itself, whether it be the law of Wonderland or, by extension, the law wherever it is encountered. Alice has already lost faith in her own search for the law of Wonderland, but then she forgets even that loss. In the final trial, where her forgotten suspicions return to become a frightful apperception of the intransigent chaos underlying her artificial world, Alice is moved to her only salvation—a complete and active denial of the horrible, unacceptable truth. In these last two chapters, after all the destruction of the old grounds of order, the only thing left is the hollow form of things. The trial now appears in its true light: since the world in which the trial takes place is without order or meaning, the trial is itself a pointless formality, another nonsensical game without rules and without a winner. And when Alice is herself again drawn into the mad proceedings and forced to participate, her open rebellion is, arguably, inevitable.

That Alice at the beginning of the trial has not yet abandoned completely her old cherished faith in order is revealed in a number of ways. The narrator tells us that "Alice had never been in a court of justice before, but she had read about them in books, and she was quite pleased to find that she knew the name of nearly everything there" (*W*, 86). Once more, Alice persists in viewing the underground bedlam from an "in-the-world" perspective. Part of the witty comedy here naturally derives from the fact that many adult readers have been in a court of law: they know that this Wonderland court is an outlandish travesty (especially when it is called a "court of justice"). Yet they also sense that at the core there is a great deal of similarity between "real" trials above ground and this insanely unjust trial of the Knave of Hearts underground. They also sense the ironic significance of Alice's confusion of names and meanings, her comfort in finding that she can *name* the items in the court—another illustration of Wonderland's incessant attack on humankind's groundless but persistent linguistic habits, intensified when the narrator remarks with sly irony that Alice was rather proud of her ability to name everything in the court, "for she thought, and rightly too, that very few little girls of her age knew the meaning of it all" (*W*, 86). An even more important result of Alice's "in-the-world" approach to the trial is that she will again be frustrated, this time by the fact that while the Wonderland trial is similar in outward form to "real" trials, it characteristically ignores or subverts all the significant principles.

The title of the final chapter, "Alice's Evidence," has multiple meanings. Literally, Alice is forced here to participate actively in the insanity of Wonderland by giving "evidence," even though she has now grown so large that she can at any second rebel and end the trial if she so desires. More important, Alice in this last scene acquires the "evidence" she needs in order to make her final decision about Wonderland. At first Alice reacts with fear; when she is called to the stand, she cries out, " 'Here!' . . . quite forgetting in the flurry of the moment how large she had grown in the last few minutes" (*W*, 92). Along with this fear, however, is a growing sense of the meaninglessness of the trial (and thus, she thinks, of all Wonderland). Hence, when she looks over the jurymen's shoulders and sees the nonsense they are writing, Alice says to herself, "It doesn't matter a bit" (*W*, 93). Here she is becoming just as subversive toward Wonderland as Wonderland has been toward her and her above-ground principles. Soon Alice is courageously contradicting the King and Queen openly: " 'That *proves* his guilt, of course,' said the Queen: 'so, off with—.' 'It doesn't prove anything of the sort!' said Alice" (*W*, 94). And after the White Rabbit reads his major piece of "evidence" against the Knave of Hearts, the mad poem full of unclear pronoun references, Alice daringly states aloud, " 'If any one of them [the jury] can explain it,' . . . (she had grown so large in the last few minutes that she wasn't a bit afraid of interrupting him [the King]), 'I'll give him sixpence. *I* don't believe there's an atom of meaning in it' " (*W*, 95). Finally, when the Queen asserts, "Sentence first—verdict afterwards," Alice says loudly, "Stuff and nonsense!" The Queen turns purple with rage, Alice actively denies the Queen's demand to be silent with a forceful "I won't!" and the whole underground adventure explodes and disintegrates (*W*, 96–97).

One can seen here, in the progression from Alice's thinking "to herself" to her final words said "loudly" and her absolute refusal to keep silent, that part of her rebellion rests on her growing ability to assign the proper names, to speak the necessary words—to give the necessary "evidence." In chapter 8 Alice was outwardly polite while she inwardly said, "They're only a pack of cards, after all." Here at the end, she is completely open, and she terminates her nightmarish adventures with her own weapon of destruction, her loudly proclaimed, "You're nothing but a pack of cards!" (*W*, 97).

Alice's final, overt rejection of Wonderland, her flight from the frightful anarchy of the world underneath the grounds of common consciousness, is a symbolic rejection of mad sanity in favor of the sane madness of ordinary existence. Perhaps it is best to view the normal conscious mind as an automatic filtering and ordering mechanism that protects us from seeing the world in all its chaotic wonder and glory—at least it seems best to view the mind this way when we attempt an explanation of the serious meanings that emerge from the delicious, sprightly wit and warm humor of *Alice's Adventures in Wonderland*. When Alice at last names her tormentors a mere pack of cards and thereby ends her underground journey, her mind by that very assertion imposes an artificial but effective order upon that which can never be organically ordered. By the time Alice and the reader reach this last scene in Wonderland it should be quite obvious to all that language itself is a woefully inadequate construct, a mere "pack of cards" that can be made to represent whatever its user chooses. Yet it is by this construct that Alice preserves her sanity and identity. She uses words to put all Wonderland into a category of manufactured, nonhuman, arbitrary entities—playthings, "a pack of cards." Insane as her naming act may be in terms of what Wonderland has demonstrated, it provides her with the means to dispel her nightmare vision and thus protect her from the dangers of complete perception.

Alice has thus come full circle: her mad curiosity has led her to the vision of absurdity; her failure to deal with that absurdity has led her to dismay; and her instinct for survival, assured identity, and sanity has led her to escape from her final horrifying perception. In the end, then, Alice refuses to join the mad dance to which her overweening curiosity has brought her.

Alice's Adventures in Wonderland is not a piece of formal philosophy; it is, instead, a comic myth of humanity's insoluble problem of meaning in an ultimately meaningless world. Thus, the fact that Alice herself is unaware of the significance of her journey to the end of night and unaware of her reasons for finally denying the validity of her vision is by no means a flaw in the book. Alice, as the mythical representative of all her fellows above ground, acts appropriately and appropriately is unaware of the full meaning of her actions. Although Alice's quest for meaning is unfulfilled and she consciously learns nothing, she does survive because an instinctual "lesson" takes over at the moment of supreme danger. Unlike the artificial, contingent, illusory lessons of her nursery reading, schoolroom, elders, and society and unlike the horrible, deconstructive lessons that Wonderland implicitly teaches, the innate and unconscious drive for identity and self-preservation cannot be perverted by either Wonderland or the world above it. The question is not whether this drive is a valid principle, but whether it is pragmatically sound. In *Wonderland* it is. And upon its pragmatic soundness rests the validity of all the other illusory above-ground principles and conventions. Alice's quest for reasonable experience whisks her back to her only possible, albeit artificial, world where the ultimately irrational often makes life sane.

Thus, *Wonderland* is paradoxically both a denial and an affirmation of constructed order—a kind of comically disguised catharsis of what can never be truly purged but what must, for sanity's sake, be periodically purged in jest, fantasy, and dream. The frightening and funny Wonderland creatures and their world are not a pack of cards, after all. They are, so to speak, more real than so-called reality. But waking life, as most of us know it, must function as if they are unreal, as if chaos is amusing "nonsense"—as if Lewis Carroll's deft revisions in his title from "under" to "wonder" and "ground" to "land" merely constitute adjustments for the sake of euphony rather than carefully chosen shifts from stark realism to sweet fantasy, sugarcoating a pill too bitter to swallow.

On the surface, then, *Alice in Wonderland* is clearly not true to ordinary experience. Yet even on the surface, the book is certainly true to an extraordinary experience familiar to us all, the dream. For many apparently nonsensical elements of *Alice,* like timelessness, spaceless-ness, and the fusion of discrete entities, are, as modern psychology has demonstrated, what lie just below the surface of rational, organized consciousness and what we experience every night in dreams. And while Alice's dream seems to fail to come to a satisfying conclusion, leaving unsolved the problem of the disorder beneath manufactured order, what I have argued here says that this is not so—that *Alice's Adventures in Wonderland* solves the problem by a kind of alogical dreamwork affirmation of humankind's artificially constructed universe. Whether or not every reader's unconscious desire for order can be satisfied by this extrarational solution is an unanswerable and finally an irrelevant ques-tion. Alice's unconscious is what matters, and it is here that the conclu-sion is satisfactory. After waking, Alice runs off for tea because "it's getting late" (this after the silly White Rabbit and the timeless Mad Tea-Party!), "thinking while she ran, as well she might, what a wonderful dream it had been" (*W,* 98), completely at ease in her own mis-remembering, completely secure in her mad but possible world above the underground chaos of Wonderland.

5

Through the Looking-Glass: Alice Becomes an I*

"I don't want to be anybody's prisoner. I want to be a Queen."

One way to account for the remarkably widespread and enduring appeal of Carroll's *Alices* is to recognize that they speak to us, covertly, about our most pressing and persistent doubts and fears; that they speak, moreover, in the perennial symbolic language of myth and dream—a language whose archetypical features have preoccupied many of our century's most provocative thinkers, Sigmund Freud, Carl Jung, and Joseph Campbell among them. In matter-of-fact narratives rendered precisely through a limpid prose style simple enough for little children (and hence for easy translation), Carroll reproduces with uncanny vividness the actual "mad" experience of the fantastic dream state. As if unmediated by a waking consciousness, the *Alices*, with their ostensibly free-flowing, indeterminate dream structures and their primal dream symbolism, resonate with the aura of transcendent but elusive truth typically associated with uncensored dreams. Thus, the *Alices* are permeated with a haunting sense of mythic applicability to life that seems to defy the boundaries of geography, culture, class, or age.

*This chapter is based on "Through the Looking-Glass: Alice Becomes an I," *Victorians Institute Journal* 15 (1987): 1–16.

Through the Looking Glass: Alice Becomes an I

However, Alice's adventures underground and on the other side of the looking-glass must not be regarded as elusive parts of a *single* dream that deals in an indeterminate, plotless, and random manner with all life in general, a dream that precludes detailed explication or precise localization in time or place. For Carroll's accounts of Alice's two dreams are of course finally not vague dreams, but highly wrought, deliberately structured works of art rooted in a particular historical setting and culture. They are, moreover, two separate and distinct literary entitites, each dealing in its own peculiar fashion with, for the most part, substantially different aspects of life, each rendering its own insights into, first, bourgeois mid-Victorian England and then into many societies and cultures beyond that particular home base.

This means, among other things, that *Through the Looking-Glass* demands its own critical reading, one that respects its artistic autonomy as well as its close relationships with *Wonderland,* its seemingly universal aspects as well as its many specific connections to Dodgson's middle-class milieu, to his beloved Alice Liddell, and to the process of growing up in his own world of dizzying change and ominously shifting perceptions of truth, meaning, and human value. Many of Carroll's best critics have treated *Wonderland* and *Through the Looking-Glass* as if they constituted one seamless text. Despite the fact that the books were composed some six or seven years apart, that their plots, settings, and themes differ radically, and that their heroine manifests in the two sets of adventures two distinctly different stages of human development, little of the massive critical attention devoted over the past 70 years to Carroll's masterpieces treats the two as clearly separate entities. The preceding interpretation of *Wonderland* and the following one of *Through the Looking-Glass* try to do just that.

Alice's underground adventures, as I have already suggested, can be understood as the bad dreams of an infantile psyche. Full of random primal fears—the terrors of going out like a spent candle into sheer nothingness, of suddenly losing one's head, of being annihilated by monstrous, inexplicable grown-up creatures who come and go unpredictably; the dread of irresistible raw separation and permanent abandonment, of uncontrollable growth in an ever-constricting womb—

Wonderland itself offers the feeble incipient ego no shelter or hope, no means for mastering its own condition. Poor little Alice's only effective defense against this maddening dream reality lies in flight, in retreat to her former childish innocence. Her sudden awakening answers her final screams of "Stuff and nonsense!" and "You're nothing but a pack of cards!" with the safety of a sister's motherly lap and the adult conventions of middle-class Victorian tea. Awake, secure, and no longer bereft, Alice at the end of her adventures in Wonderland remains unaware of the new power she has just exercised: those first verbal assertions of a fragile, budding self to externalize the horrible forces of its own disintegration, to reject its nightmarish fears, and to begin making sense of chaos by imposing upon the hostile powers of dark nonsense some manageable human design. When at the end of *Wonderland* Alice breaks off her infantile nightmares and returns to the protective care of her loving sister, she is almost back at the beginning. She becomes again a docile, dependent, unthreatened inhabitant of the simple light, cured for the moment of her dangerous curiosity about self and the dark underworld beneath the safe grounds of innocence—a serene Eve-child returned by her protective creator to a bourgeois paradise of infantile stasis and security. Her last thoughts about Wonderland, her memory of dream adventures so frightening she once considered them "enough to drive one crazy" (*W*, 46), come merely to this: "what a wonderful dream it had been" (*W*, 98).

ALICE GROWING UP

Alice's adventures behind the looking-glass, on the other hand, constitute the dream of a much more mature psyche, one well on its way to satisfactory integration and a conscious grasp of fear, time, evil, and death. Carroll's sequel enacts the myth of an Alice *after* the fall, a relatively experienced heroine who knows something of underground and mortality, something of her self and the rules of the game—an older, wiser heroine who has already learned to see herself objectively and to externalize and manage much of the destructive power inherent in her ancient fears. Replete with instances of Alice's cool dominance over her condition and over the once all-threatening creatures of her vivid infantile imagination, the *Looking-Glass* dream comically celebrates the budding mastery of an individuated psyche assuming self-control and a measure of autonomy, a confident Alice rehearsing her independent self in preparation for a rapidly approaching adulthood. Assuming the role played by her elder sister in the frame story of *Wonderland,* Alice alone in the frame story of *Looking-Glass* plays motherly mistress to her own real kitten. And within the *Looking-Glass* adventures themselves, as the self-possessed, indulgent caretaker of the weak, incompetent, silly and infantile creatures of her still lively imagination, Alice plays the integrated self ready and eager for independent queenhood outside the psychic womb.[1]

Obviously, in the passage from underground to looking-glass, Alice has changed critically. But the only effective way readers can know the events of her change or imagine the thematic substance of Carroll's unwritten account of it (call it, say, "Alice's Adventures *between* Underground and Chessboard") is obliquely, by conjecture. However, a reliable basis for such conjecture is readily available: in *Through the Looking-Glass* we can catch some clear dream reflections of those unchronicled but crucial earlier stages of Alice's development—those stages of self-discovery and individuation when the inchoate, underground forces of elemental fear and self-preservation coalesce into a stable, public self, and when that self then dotes dangerously on itself in the narcissistic stasis of a new, more complex version of infantile consciousness.

To reflect those unchronicled stages of Alice's transformation, Carroll's *Looking-Glass* text depends principally on a series of subtle elaborations of a single specific device, the mirror. Just what readers should have expected, even if they did not know that the adventures had been composed by an author notoriously obsessed with inversions and reversals in words, mirrors, mirror-writing, photography, logic, and life itself—that shy, respectable, and very grownup Oxford don who, in order to conceal his own child's play, invented for his subversive comic fantasies a pen name that is, in essence, simply a backwards mirror image of his adult name above ground and on the outer side of the looking-glass.[2]

What we typically see in a mirror, besides our own image, is what lies behind us—in a sense, not where we are going, but where we have been. As the White Queen of *Through the Looking-Glass* tells Alice, the "one great advantage" of living backwards as she does—that is, of moving through the looking-glass to what lies behind you in space and time—is "that one's memory works both ways" (*L,* 150). Dodgson's own memory often seemed to work "both ways": at the same time he thought often of his approaching death and the sadly unavoidable maturation of the young girls whom he loved for their "pure" youthfulness, he also kept detailed records of his past life, desperately trying to hold back the passage of time because he saw so acutely what lay ahead. By means of such devices as his meticulous Letter Register, his exact diary entries, his lists of now-matured child friends, his photographic records of once-beloved little girls, and his records of luncheons he had given, he worshipped his own memories. Indeed, his curiously religious opening lines to *Wonderland* beg Alice to take his "childish story" and lay it in "Memory's mystic band," as if its chief value is as a kind of religious memorial to the past that always lies behind us.

Alice's journey through the looking-glass also "works both ways," constituting not only a rapid moving forward, but also a moving backward, recapitulating what she has in her psychological development already passed through. Similarly, in his title *Through the Looking-Glass,* Carroll, like his childish White Queen, also has it "both ways," characteristically enacted in an elaborated pun on the word *through:* his (older) Alice progresses *through* (beyond) the mere reflections of the mirror, away from him and into real grownup life; but at the same time she relives, *through* (by means of) looking-glass reflections, what already lies behind her, recapitulating the childish stages of her development, the life she had led before crossing over the mantelpiece and becoming a queen, the unrecorded adventures of a young Alice that Dodgson/Carroll had already lost. In Carroll's formulation the mirror is therefore simultaneously a snare and a means of escape: it all depends on what one makes of the seemingly innocuous preposition *through.*

However, it must be stressed at the outset that literal mirrors never appear behind Carroll's looking-glass. Before her new chess-game adventures begin, Alice has by and large already passed through the critical mirror phase of her development in which the young self fixates on itself in a narcissistic circle of self-discovery iterated and reiterated. Her easy passage across the mantelpiece and through the mirror at the beginning of *Through the Looking-Glass* serves primarily as the emblem of her past maturation. It is appropriate, therefore, that an explicit mirror appears only once and only briefly at the outer surface, at the very opening of her new adventures. Nevertheless, the implicit idea of mirror dominates this dream, reflecting, by means of a number of childish looking-glass creatures, where Alice has already journeyed, reflecting too in a number of mirror reversals the themes of narcissism, maturation, self-realization, and selflessness that inform Carroll's last tribute to Alice Liddell—who, at the first publication of *Through the Looking-Glass,* was nearly 20 years old and thus rapidly approaching her majority.

STRUCTURAL DIFFERENCES

Before examining several of these elaborations of the mirror motif in *Through the Looking-Glass,* it is instructive to consider a related matter—a graphic, essential difference between the structural elements of the two *Alice* books. In *Wonderland* the dominant geometric pattern is distinctly circular and static. Like the encircling womb memories of psychic infancy, *Wonderland* enfolds Alice's disturbing dreams in circular, idyllic peace, in a narrative frame that turns back on itself and ends where it begins—with a stable tableau of a sheltered mother-child dyad nestled within a structurally static, centripetal frame story. When *Wonderland* ends with thoughtless little Alice running off, late to tea, we are returned full circle to the tale's beginning and to the seemingly innocuous White Rabbit darting—also late—down the fateful, yonic rabbit hole, carrying us back, in turn, to the adventures' central episode, the timeless Mad Tea-Party filled with endless circular motion and yet forever still—there at the structural and thematic center of Alice's underground journey. In other words, in terms of psychological development, Alice seems to go nowhere in her dreams of Wonderland. She ends the adventures once again secure in her sister's nurturing care, undifferentiated and safe from the terrifying, erratic dreams she has just experienced. The psychological results of her adventures are effectively symbolized by Alice's own direct involvement in the story's dominant circle imagery: joining a pointless circular caucus race where everyone wins or an endless circular tea party where the food never runs out. These scenes portray infantile images of that earliest stage of consciousness before time and linear progression; the rich, passive, static, undifferentiated and fluid world of the nurturing womb; the concentric id logic of fetal desire: "Beautiful Soup."

PLAYING THE GAME

Conversely, *Through the Looking-Glass*—structured, as Carroll claimed in the preface to the 1895 edition, "strictly in accordance with the laws of the game [of chess]"—is in many ways linear, progressive, and goal-oriented, based as it is on the straight lines and squares of an actual chessboard and (loosely) on the predictable linear movements of the chess pieces, particularly the movements of one little determined pawn as it marches straight across its five squares to its queening. And the sequel's heroine, now aware of the significance of living in space and time (regardless of their ultimate relativity), is decidedly active, logical, and self-directed, making her efficient moves deliberately, advancing on her own impending queenhood and chess victory swiftly and surely. For example, even in the *Looking-Glass* scene that comes closest to the epistemological anxiety of Alice's identity-threatening adventures underground, the brief episode in the wood where things have no names (chapter 3), Alice reveals a determination to move forward characteristic of a heroine much more mature and sophisticated than the confused little Alice of *Wonderland*. Despite her timidity over entering such a dark wood, "she made up her mind to go on: 'for I certainly won't go *back,*' she thought to herself." For "this was the only way to the Eighth Square" and her queening (*L,* 135). The developmental advantages of playing the game, in spite of Dodgson's deep doubts about the (constructed) nature of reality and in spite of his distaste for the Rugby school of his youth and its emphasis on violent, but character-building games, are here made evident. As Kathleen Blake observes in her discussion of Alice's game playing in *Looking-Glass,* "By asserting her own will she at the same time acts in accordance with the rules of actual chess, which are unmuddled, stable, and hence fair enough to make victory possible."[3] For, as Blake says, "the main thing [in games] is to fix the perimeter and the internal relationship structure, the terms and rules, of a game system, and make these stick. Then the universe will be secure (what Carroll calls certain), and one will enjoy the freedom of that security."[4]

Similarly, Alice's response to forgetting her own name in the dark wood of no names sounds a keynote of her grown-up determination throughout *Looking-Glass:* "And now who am I?" she asks, as if suddenly regressing to Wonderland where this insistent underground question never gets answered. Alice's added "And now," however, deftly marks the difference between her utter childishness in *Wonderland* and her relativistic, businesslike maturity behind the looking-glass: For one thing, "And now" here seems to allude to the fact that identity is time-specific, contingent—who one is depends on when, as well as where, one is. Furthermore, Alice here valiantly struggles to answer the question herself, and to answer it in terms of her past: "I *will* remember, if I can! I'm determined to do it!" (*L,* 136). A far cry— in substance, voice, and expression—from Alice's comparatively passive and helpless reactions to similar setbacks in the completely timeless, spaceless underground of *Wonderland.*

Thus advanced to a new developmental stage, the Alice of *Looking-Glass* is ready for the final moves ahead that will, by what Carroll calls "the laws of the game," enable her to assume the freedom and strength of a queen, the chessboard's most powerful, mobile, self-sufficient piece. Her matured understanding can reach into fields far beyond those available to the primal consciousness—indeed, can engage the whole world. When, for example, from a "little hill" she first looks down upon the new dream realm neatly and logically laid out for those old enough to master the rules of chess, she declares "in a tone of delight. . . . 'It's a great huge game of chess that's being played—all over the world' " (*L*, 125–26). Based on the strict linearity and arbitrary, unchanging rules of chess, on the progressive motions of a knowledgeable player advancing consciously through a timed series of well-defined moves to limited but attainable power and self-sufficiency, these last dream adventures trace Alice's final eager steps toward the victory of competent selfhood in the worldly games waking grown-ups play above the grounds of their infantile (if often valid) fears, as well as beyond the stultifying, deceptive mirrors of their static, childish self-love. Teaching his little-girl friends the moves and rules of chess apparently marked for Dodgson a noteworthy stage in their maturation: even the youngest of his friends could play cards and simple word games, but chess was clearly an adult game that could put his cleverest young protégées on something like an equal footing with their grown-up opponents.

Immediately after realizing the game nature of the world in which she finds herself behind the mirror, Alice says to the Red Queen, "How I wish I could be one of the [chess pieces]. I wouldn't mind being a Pawn . . . though of course I should like to be a Queen best." The Queen replies, "That's easily managed" (*L*, 126). Almost a mirror reversal of the generally useless, often exasperating advice Alice received from the maddening creatures of Wonderland, this preliminary advice from the Red Queen is accurate and eminently useful: it will serve Alice well behind the looking-glass. Alice can indeed "manage" now[5]—first, because she is mature and competent enough to play and win in an adult game like chess (contrast here the infantile, ruleless, and winless games of her adventures underground; contrast also the *Wonderland* playing-card motif that represents chance in a one-dimensional field rather than skill in the more or less two-dimensional field of the *Looking-Glass* chess pieces);[6] second, and more significant, because she begins her new journey with a self-conception so firm and stable, she is no longer in serious danger of losing her way for long, of becoming ensnared, whether it be in the unprogressive circularity of early infancy or in the later circularity of childish self-worship.

RISING TO HIGHER THINGS

Yet in her straight and purposeful march to queenhood and victory Alice does encounter plenty of circularity and self-mirroring—now, however, outside herself in the creatures of her imagination, which she swiftly leaves in her wake. In a rich variety of configurations, many of these Looking-Glass creatures repeat (as if in an infinite regression of mirror reflections of mirror reflections) a single narcissistic, circular pattern, a static mirroring of self. And at the very center of these adventures sits the unstable Humpty Dumpty, that imperious, egocentric, spherical big baby who, childishly believing himself "master," unknowingly teeters on the brink of his own inevitable fall and dissolution. Humpty Dumpty can be considered the emblem for the self-centered Looking-Glass personality: like him, almost everyone the shrewd young manager Alice meets beyond the looking-glass is an infantile, permanent prisoner of the mirror through which she has already passed. The Looking-Glass creatures are symbols of her former identities, dream projections and recapitulations of the childish stages she has put behind herself. Indeed, her Looking-Glass journey loosely reenacts that former passage, and during her progress through "that great huge game of chess," in dream play she once again leaves each of these static creatures behind her, frozen forever in the nursery rhymes of her earlier development. Like pieces in a game she has already won—parts of her former psychic self, still in some sense operative, but now subdued, perceived as childish, and thus under her conscious control—these creatures are no longer fully alive in her, no longer capable of pulling her back to the original, undifferentiated Eden before her stable, conscious self emerged.[7]

Tennyson's *In Memoriam* (a poem Dodgson so admired that he arranged for his sisters to compile an index of it, which was published in

1862) traces the poet's spiritual journey from deep doubt to ecstatic affirmation, from self-centered, rather infantile despair and disengagement to mature reintegration with nature and society. The extremely popular poem—considered by many modern scholars a literary paradigm of the bourgeois Victorian's spiritual experience—attempts to demonstrate how "men may rise on stepping-stones / Of their dead selves to higher things" (section 1, line 4). The conversion-oriented developmental pattern celebrated by Tennyson occurs repeatedly throughout Victorian literature. And in a sense, it is repeated in the *Alices*: the infantile creatures of *Through the Looking-Glass* represent Alice's "dead selves," the "stepping stones" of her underground infancy and her narcissistic childhood and early adolescence—past selves she has risen on in her drive toward self-mastery and those middle-class "higher things," like the admirable, unselfish social consciousness she demonstrates as the heroine (and eventual queen) of *Through the Looking-Glass*.

The first characters Alice meets after crossing the mantelpiece are three pairs of disheveled chess pieces—the Red King and Queen, the White King and Queen, and the "two Castles walking arm in arm" (*L*, 113). These matching doubles prefigure at the outset the self-reflecting circularity within which all the looking-glass creatures seem to exist, the mirror motif that pervades the adventures, and the mirroring symmetrical/asymmetrical field within which the text is cast and upon which Alice must play the game that lies before her.[8] Moreover, these incompetent chess characters act as foils for the nearly matured, self-possessed player Alice. Like them, all the other looking-glass creatures Alice meets are childish grown-ups; and consistent with her actions here at the beginning, Alice will almost invariably treat them like children who require her kindly attention and nurture. Hence, we are soon told in this opening scene that "Alice was very anxious to be of use"; she picks up the fallen, crying chess figures "very gently" and puts into order the untidy scene. Smoothing the King's tousled hair as she sets him "upon the table near the Queen," Alice addresses him as "my dear"—a locution often used, in the British vernacular, with small children (*L*, 114–15).

All this is of course a far cry from Alice's typically frightened reactions to insane royalty and maddening disorder in Wonderland. For here behind the looking-glass Alice makes order and acts the powerful but kindly and patient mother figure in a world of selfish, incompetent children: a self-composed Victorian young lady who chooses to act with the solicitude and noblesse oblige required of her by her upper-middle-class ethos. With the aplomb of an accomplished actress, Alice now plays beautifully the grownup, culture-bearing, dominant role in which her elevated social position has cast her,[9] demonstrating, in a mirror reversal of the creatures' narcissistic behavior, that she, at least, has already traveled through the looking-glass, that in a world full of selfish, infantile, incompetent creatures— whatever their chronological ages—she, at least, can see beyond her own reflection and can act with what her class considered authentic, mature altruism.

For while discerning the reflection of one's separate self (in the mirror or elsewhere) marks a major stage in the maturational process, it is of course not the ultimate aim of human development—certainly not for the Reverend Dodgson, nor for his original, bourgeois, Christian audience. To see beyond or through the looking-glass, to see what lies on the other side of self, to accept the human burden of caring for the world and others less fortunate, less "enlightened," or less powerful than onself—this for Dodgson/Carroll was the ideological imperative for a mature human existence. That his Alice has come, by the beginning of *Through the Looking-Glass,* to accept such a burden is at once both her triumph and, it seems, an important source of the widespread admiration *Through the Looking-Glass* continues to provoke.

TWEEDLEDUM AND TWEEDLEDEE

Not long after the opening episode with the chess pieces, Alice encounters another set of mirror images, the identical, identically reversed twins Tweedledum and Tweedledee. But even before meeting this "couple of great schoolboys" (as she refers to these men-children), she has already realized that they are not the two separate selves they think themselves to be. Just before the meeting, Alice has spotted their two mirroring signposts: TO TWEEDLEDUM'S HOUSE and TO THE HOUSE OF TWEEDLEDEE. Wise now to the ways of signs, mirrors, and narcissistic self-deception, Alice declares, "I do believe . . . that they live in the *same* house!" This realization hints at the measure of her matured understanding about human identity—a topic that has puzzled her from almost the beginning of her first adventures underground. For although the baby-ish Tweedles in their blatant self-love consider themselves two separate creatures, Alice seems to understand that they are deluded like the self-enamored Narcissus of ancient myth. Moreover, Alice also thinks here about her own process of perception when she immediately adds, "I wonder I never thought of that before" (*L*, 137). Such contemplation and self-contemplation represent a mirror reversal of the Tweedles' permanent infantile delusion about their identities. Alice accurately sees herself here as two different people, different because time has changed her and matured her understanding ("I [now] wonder" vs. "I [then] never thought"). At some point in her past, she realizes, she too was incapable of distinguishing a doubled mirror identity from a truly doubled reality. Indeed, back in Wonderland she was, as the narrator told us, "fond of pretending to be two people" (*W*, 12)—a sign of precociousness perhaps, but not a sign of mature consciousness and psychic integration. And that fondness, like the (conjectured) foolish, fond self-love of her later (unrecorded) stages of development, has apparently been overcome in her growth, in her fall from circular, self-satisfied innocence to a new recognition of selfhood and otherness in a world of time and change. Now like a mature adult, Alice can truly "wonder" about her self as an evolving, changing entity living in time, rather than a static, permanently infantile one caught in its own timeless mirror image—like the immortal Tweedle couple thinking of itself as two separate grown-ups when, in fact, it is for all intents and purposes a single infantile child trapped in a mirror reflection, forever frozen in the immutable text of a well-worn nursery rhyme.[10]

In a parody of infantile selfishness, the Tweedles (Alice thinks of them as "fat little men") play out their predetermined nursery-rhyme battle (presumably ad infinitum)—all, appropriately, over "a nice new RATTLE" (*L*, 146). Neatly encapsulating the twins' essential contribution to the book's unfolding anatomy of static narcissism, Alice characterizes them as "selfish things!" (*L*, 146), but of course not out loud: the solicitous, motherly, well-mannered Alice consistently avoids hurting the delicate feelings of the childish Looking-Glass creatures. It is seeing them as "things" that allows Alice—and the reader—to distinguish between the human state beyond the mirror and the less-than-human state inside the mirror. As infants, they are indeed still like things, like mere projections of the id, while Alice, as her well-phrased remarks here indicate, is already a full-fledged human being, a relatively self-willed agent, a nearly mature woman now capable of treating the Tweedles for just what they are—silly mirror babies fighting an endless, harmless mock-battle over a mere rattle: " 'Of course you agree to have a battle?' Tweedledum said. . . . 'I suppose so,' the other sulkily replied. . . . '[O]nly *she* must help us to dress up, you know' " (*L*, 147).

Alice proceeds to humor the Tweedles with motherly patience. Again acting the competent grownup, she dresses the two great babies and gently ministers to their needs, avoiding at all costs wounding their fragile egos. Reacting to a particularly nonsensical remark of Tweedledee's, for example, she manages to turn her loud involuntary laughter "into a cough, for fear," we are told, "of hurting his feelings" (*L*, 147). Alice's gentle nurturing response even goes so far as to approximate the final developmental stage that awaits her—the maternal, generative, teaching stage: fruitlessly she attempts to teach these selfish Tweedles some of the elements of mature perception, selflessness and self-control—" 'And all that about a rattle!' said [the motherly] Alice, still hoping to make them a *little* ashamed of fighting for such a trifle" (*L*, 148).

The pattern continues. For example, in chapter 5, "Wool and Water," Alice, again acting the part of the discreet and powerful older woman with the still childish, disheveled, incompetent, and self-centered White Queen, gently dresses her and diplomatically manages the social encounter: "Alice felt if there was to be any conversation at all, she must manage it herself" (L, 149). (Much later, in chapter 9, the Red Queen orders Alice to smooth the White Queen's hair and sing her a soothing *lullaby* [L, 196]).[11] The White Queen's childishness is apparently the result, as she herself admits, of "living backwards"—an allusion to, among other things, the regressiveness Alice has at this stage overcome and put behind her into unconsciousness: " 'Living backwards!' Alice repeated in great astonishment. 'I never heard of such a thing!' " (L, 150), despite the fact that in her underground adventures she had experienced much that could justifiably be called "living backwards"—almost to the point of "going out altogether, like a candle" (W, 12).[12]

In chapter 8, "It's My Own Invention," Alice again plays the indulgent and nurturing mother figure—this time to the aged White Knight, a laughably innocent, senile figure in his second childhood who keeps tumbling off his horse. In a deliciously naturalistic touch, Carroll allows Alice to lose, but only for a brief moment, her mature patience with the Knight's childish incompetence, suggesting he belongs on a child's nursery horse, a hint he characteristically misses:

> "It's too ridiculous!" cried Alice, losing all her patience this time. "You ought to have a wooden horse on wheels, that you ought!"
>
> "Does that kind go smoothly?" the Knight asked in a tone of great interest, clasping his arms round the horse's neck as he spoke, just in time to save himself from tumbling off again.
>
> "Much more smoothly than a live horse," Alice said, with a little scream of laughter, in spite of all she could do to prevent it.
>
> "I'll get one," the Knight said thoughtfully to himself. "One or two—several." (L, 184)

HUMPTY DUMPTY'S NARCISSISM

Perhaps most important in this pattern of child-adult reversal and self-mirroring narcissism traced in this discussion is chapter 6, "Humpty Dumpty," the chapter that serves as the structural center of Alice's 12-chapter adventures behind the mirror. For in Humpty Dumpty Alice meets the reductio ad absurdum of circular narcissism. The spherical Humpty Dumpty, for one thing, believes himself master because he masters words; but what he is ridiculously unaware of is that, like a number of other infantile prisoners of the Looking-Glass world, his very existence, the permanence and integrity of his self is "mastered" by the words of an unchanging text, the nursery rhyme that comprises his only identity, his sole claim on existence. Furthermore, lurking behind Humpty Dumpty's childish bravado is Alice's mature awareness that his fall and disintegration are inevitable and that, unlike Alice's self after her disastrous fall down the rabbit hole, his can never be reconstructed or developed. For his whole existence is merely the fixed mirror image of a predetermined and unchanging verbal text, the last lines of which Alice, with typical polite circumspection, recites *silently* to herself: "All the King's horses / And all the King's men / Couldn't put Humpty in his place again." Immediately, however, Alice realizes that the "last line is much too long for the poetry" (*L,* 159). Her doubts here about her memory and the efficiency of her own mental processes offer a neat contrast to Humpty Dumpty's invariable and childish self-assurance. Her compassionate silence stems from her mature realization that the last line is too long to reflect the short life expectancy of an unbalanced egg on a wall.

"Some people ... have no more sense than a baby," Humpty Dumpty tells Alice when she begins the episode by inadvertently remarking "how exactly like an egg he is" (*L,* 159). Humpty's rude remark, of course, like so much else in this pivotal episode, constitutes an ironic mirror reversal. For it is Humpty Dumpty, not the obviously discreet and civil Alice, who has "no more sense than a baby." Indeed, Humpty has so little sense that he remains, like a baby, blissfully unaware of the fact that, as Alice tells him, "one can't help growing older" (*L,* 162) and blissfully ignorant of the dire consequences of an egg perched precariously on a wall: the impending fall that will destroy his identity forever, a fall ironically guaranteed by rhyme and by words, the element he officiously claims to "master."

Like the self-love of Narcissus, Humpty Dumpty's comically exaggerated self-esteem is finally incorrigible—and fatal. Moreover, he fits perfectly into the self-worshiping mirror motif on which Carroll's narrative depends. His name and the name of his chapter repeat the verbal doubling found throughout *Looking-Glass*—for example, in the two previous chapter titles, "Wool and Water" and "Tweedledum and Tweedledee," in other key words with doubled letters like "mirror" and "looking-glass," and in the name Alice Liddell (a name that ends the book in the closing poem's acrostic spelling of Alice's full name) or the pen name that seems to mirror hers, Lewis Carroll. In addition, Humpty Dumpty caricatures the egocentricity of the earliest phases of the mirror stage—a babyish nursery-rhyme figure so infantile that he is literally an egg, a prenatal sphere that turns upon itself in a sort of permanent self-absorption, a throwback to the womb circularity of the rabbit hole and the amniotic pool of tears. Completely, egotistically unconscious of his imprisonment in a simple nursery rhyme—that is, in the timeless developmental stage that precedes conscious self-knowledge and self-command—unconscious too of his own precarious state and unavoidable, impending disintegration, Humpty represents the solipsism Alice repeatedly encounters and leaves behind in her accelerating rush toward self-consciousness and the freedom (as well as the burdens) it confers.

Furthermore, Humpty Dumpty's childish ignorance of the way human exchanges require a recognition of other selves and of meanings beyond willful self-assertion makes him, in both linguistic and developmental terms, a lonely, helpless figure imprisoned by a ludicrously circular theoretical approach to the pragmatic question of human communication (a figure we sometimes encounter in real-life academic philosophers and theoreticians). Alice, on the other hand, displays in their encounter the mature sense of otherness and altruism that distinguishes her from all the infantile creatures trapped forever in their texts behind the looking-glass: Alice responds to Humpty Dumpty's outrageous insults by saying "nothing," for she doesn't, as the narrator tells us, "want to begin another argument" (*L*, 162). And in the conversation with Humpty Dumpty about the meaning of the word *glory*, Alice demonstrates another aspect of her budding maturity. Humpty asserts that *glory* means "there's a nice knock-down argument for you!" Alice politely objects, and Humpty declares that when he uses a word it means, as he says, "just what I choose it to mean—neither more nor less" (*L,* 163). This extreme linguistic narcissism, this childish and unfounded sense of control over the world's signs and its meanings is so shocking to Alice that she wisely refrains from debating the question any longer. Humpty Dumpty, she seems to conclude, is so permanently sealed into his static self-absorption that to dispute his views would be like discussing with an infant the logic of its elemental desires.

Alice's last remarks about her encounter with Humpty Dumpty sum up her reactions to the stage of development he represents, and by extension her general reactions to the many other mirror figures of her looking-glass adventures: " 'Of all the unsatisfactory'—(she repeated this aloud, as it was a great comfort to have such a long word to say) 'of all the unsatisfactory people I *ever* met' " (*L,* 168). Indeed, in terms of Alice's own development toward psychic integrity, Humpty Dumpty *is* an extremely unsatisfactory role model, trapped as he is in a self-mirroring stage that can offer Alice no useful behavioral model to guide her in her drive toward the freedom and power of autonomous queenhood. The best, the most "satisfactory" example he offers is a negative one—an image of permanent imprisonment. But, as Alice says a little while later, "I don't want to be anybody's prisoner. I want to be a Queen" (*L,* 181).

MULTIPLE INTERPRETATIONS

The fact that in her final remarks about Humpty Dumpty Alice plays with words childishly ("it was a great comfort to have such a long word to say") and that she still needs comfort in the face of Humpty Dumpty's egocentricity and rudeness serves to indicate that the interpretation of *Through the Looking-Glass* offered here is overly schematic. Alice's progress toward maturity is not so distinct, direct, progressive, and unambiguous as this interpretation suggests. In fact, this interpretation, like the one of *Alice's Adventures in Wonderland* that precedes it, tends, in the service of a logical and progressive dissection, to shortchange Carroll's fascinating doubling and redoubling significations; his mockery and self-mockery; his fusion of infantile pleasure with mature pain, of sheer play with deep reflection; his delicious indeterminacy. For while the *Alice* books are much more than nonsense, they are often called nonsense with a certain justification, a certain sense of their tough and lovely resistance to sensible, comprehensive interpretation. And to murder to dissect that precious quality called, for want of a better term, "Carrollian nonsense," is finally inexcusable, whatever sensible arguments one can offer to justify such a critical practice.

Thus, although this interpretation of *Through the Looking-Glass* depends heavily on the premise that the creatures Alice meets behind the mirror represent varieties of infantile and childish behavior, it can be argued that they continue at the same time another pattern established in the underground adventures, serving as subversive caricatures of grown-ups and foolish, self-assured grown-up behavior. As in the complex dynamics of dream signification, Carroll's gallery of ridiculous characters in both books serves many symbolic purposes, some even contradicting others. Hence, a Humpty Dumpty can signify—for dreamer Alice or a daydreaming reader—both a foolish adult and a willful child with "no more sense than a baby." Indeed, the dream fusion of good sense and nonsense that characterizes many elements of the *Alice*s is one of the primary reasons for the books' widespread and enduring success among their immense readership, young and old.

Moreover, the interpretation offered here—unlike the *Alice* books themselves—fails to reflect the sacrifices inherent in the ego-centered developmental theory on which it rests. James R. Kincaid has demonstrated that Carroll's Alice often "upset[s] a beautiful comic game by introducing the alien concepts of linear progression to infinity, nothingness, and death"; that in rejecting the disorder of her dreams, "Alice is rejecting not only the terrifying underside of human consciousness but the liberating imagination as well"; and that the *Alice* books, among other things, depict "the child's rude and tragic haste to leave its innocence."[13]

Through the Looking Glass: Alice Becomes an I

Likewise, the rather simplistic view of who dreams Alice's dreams on which much of my interpretation of the *Alices* rests also needs adjustment. Remember that Alice herself ends her Looking-Glass adventures with what she correctly calls a "serious question": "Let's consider," she says at last to her kitty, "who it was that dreamed it all" (*L*, 208). Carroll himself, in the climactic chapter of *Through the Looking-Glass*, offers his own rather compelling answer to this fundamental question. In chapter 9, "It's My Own Invention," we witness Alice meeting her maker, for this chapter gives us in the White Knight the best mirror image, perhaps, we can ever hope to attain of that dreamer and comic genius Dodgson, alias Lewis Carroll—himself in many ways a rather childish, narcissistic figure. And it is here that we can come to realize that, among other things, Carroll's final *Alice* book allows us to see, through the looking-glass of his own devising, the shy, sometimes rather infantile inventor of Alice and her dream adventures, to see him in and as his "own invention," his own dream, as he perhaps saw himself in those many mirror reversals that fascinated him throughout his life and art. And what we see and hear in this chapter is a bittersweet farewell to the nearly 20-year-old Alice Liddell, who, as the mirror-image Alice of the book, in the same climactic chapter declares, "I don't like belonging to another person's dream" (*L*, 179), even the dream of her dear friend Mr. Dodgson.

Despite these complications and critical ambiguities, however, in her adventures behind the looking-glass, Alice has come to a mature, if not a fully satisfying, completely comforting answer to that "great puzzle" she asked early in her underground journey, "Who in the world am I?" (*W*, 15–16). Her answer, naturally, has to do with names and the naming of things—Adam's first task and since then the perplexing task of all humanity. As she tells herself emerging from the delightful *and* frightening infantile wood where things have no names, where, as in the pool of tears, she had for a moment experienced a return to timeless, preverbal, preconscious, free-flowing innocence, this time with "her dear little fellow-traveler" the Fawn, "I know my name now . . . that's *some* comfort. Alice—Alice—I won't forget it again" (*L*, 137).

6

Blessed Rage: The *Alices* and the Modern Quest for Order*

Three centuries lay between the promulgation of the Copernican theory and the publication of the *Origin of Species,* but in the sixty-odd years which have elapsed since that latter event the blows have fallen with a rapidity which left no interval for recovery. The structures which are variously known as mythology, religion, and philosophy, and which are alike in that each has as its function the interpretation of experience in terms which have human values, have collapsed under the force of successive attacks and shown themselves utterly incapable of assimilating the new stores of experience which have been dumped on the world. With increasing completeness science maps out the pattern of nature, but the latter has no relation to the pattern of human needs and feelings.... Standards are imaginary things, and yet it is extremely doubtful if man can live well, either spiritually or physically, without the belief that they are somehow real. Without them society lapses into anarchy and the individual becomes aware of an intolerable disharmony between himself and the universe.

—Joseph Wood Krutch, *The Modern Temper*[1]

If Alice's survival and development depend on her imposition of a firm, albeit artificial, vision of order and purpose on a world with no inherent principles of such order and purpose, if the stability of her self-image and sense of freedom depend on becoming a successful player of mere games, a competent actress in a constructed play uni-

*This chapter was adapted from "Blessed Rage: Lewis Carroll and the Modern Quest for Order," in *Lewis Carroll: A Celebration,* ed. Edward Guiliano (New York: Clarkson Potter, 1982), 15–25.

verse with rules, so to speak, of her own making, then the *Alices* constitute a telling dream representation of their author's own plight. Understanding this relationship between Dodgson's inner life, his legendary rage for standards and order, and the functions of order and disorder in his public imaginative works illuminates both the sources of his creative urge and the strange, curiously resilient power of the *Alices*.

A few examples will suffice. In a search for the "meaning" of the *Alices*, what can be made, for instance, of the fact that these creations of an extremely imaginative artist celebrated in particular for the indeterminacy of his free-flowing narratives are also the creations of a man who for 50 years kept a meticulous register of the contents of every letter he wrote or received—summaries of more than 98,000 letters, many of them little more than minor business notes? Or what light is shed on the *Alices* by the fact that this supremely playful comic genius who created books teeming with disorder at the same time maintained a faithful record of the many luncheons and dinners he gave throughout many years of a sociable lifetime, with diagrams showing where each guest sat and lists of just what dishes were served? Or what can we say of this trenchant satirist of obsessiveness (almost all the *Alice* creatures are chronic obsessives) who himself seriously threatened to break off relations with his publisher of 30 years' standing because he found slight printing imperfections in the eighty-four thousandth copy of one of his popular children's books, then in print for 20 years, but who denied publicly throughout his life that he had anything to do with those masterpieces of free, mad nonsense and disorder signed by Lewis Carroll?

Wherever one looks, abundant biographical evidence indicates that Dodgson was so passionately devoted to regularity in his everyday affairs that his orderliness bordered on the pathological. But he was by no means unique: most of us are acquainted with people like him, people who manifest their extraordinary need for order by obsessively regulating and standardizing their daily lives. This behavior seems to express a deep-seated anxiety about the messiness that surrounds human consciousness, an anxiety about the morally random nature of an existence that can never satisfy the human mind's need for regularity, completeness, and control. On guard against the apparently mindless chaos that threatens their beliefs, their trust, and sometimes their very sanity, people who suffer from such anxiety often fill their waking lives with artificial structure—with manufactured systems and rules their wills (like their cultures' wills) impose on the disorderly matter and events they inevitably encounter. Like the child Alice, who in the maddening anarchy of her underground dream adventures persists in citing and looking for "rules," these devotees of order continually apply artifical constructs and systems to tidy up and temporarily regularize what their unconscious minds recognize as permanent chaos—the endlessly incomplete, absurd, "dreadful confusion" (L, 204) that underlies our rationalized, futilely constructed, so-called waking world.

Scientific studies demonstrating the strict mechanical order inherent in nature, like Darwin's revolutionary explanations of nature's puzzling randomness, variation, and waste (*The Origin of Species* was published less than three years before Dodgson told his first *Alice* story to Alice Liddell and her sisters in 1862), cannot even begin to dispel such people's desperate sense of underlying anarchy. Indeed, these vexed souls are likely to find in visions like Darwin's further evidence of ultimate moral chaos; for such amoral, unprogressive, and strictly mechanical order in nature offers little human comfort, little or no power to resolve the anxieties modern men and women often suffer in contemplating the morally meaningless process that is nature and their only home. Instead of finding in Darwinian and post-Darwinian science some solution to the metaphysical vexations of apparently random natural variety, these obsessively orderly people—and by no means are they always scientifically naive—might very well find there objective, daytime corroborations of their worst nightmares: a chilling panorama of the pointless, mindless, inescapable mechanisms in which science has now placed them firmly and forever. And, consequently, they might easily find themselves, in their need for a corresponding moral pattern, for individual or collective human significance, terrifyingly alone—powerless aliens in a careless, indifferent, absurd universe. When Alice in her subterranean Wonderland cries because she is, as she says, "so *very* tired of being all alone here!" (*W,* 17), she pines not only for the human companionship she has lost, but also for some familiar signposts of intelligible order that her fellow humans dream or construct for themselves in their darkness above nature's ultimate emptiness. The religious and metaphysical assumptions that once answered the basic human need for orderly, complete, and permanent explanations and reasons beyond the reach of reason had thinned out and vanished for a great number of Victorian intellectuals during their lifetimes, destroyed by a natural, innocent, childlike curiosity like Darwin's—and like Alice's. The resulting God-less void was terrifying. It still is.

Thus, the broadly operative teleological vision that found or mythologized an orderly metaphysical structure within nature's bewildering multiplicity and waste was swept away in the nineteenth century by modern science hitting its full stride, an inescapable science that now began, decades before the publication of *The Origin of Species,* to demonstrate conclusively the true cold order of nature. Like religion, natural history could no longer serve as a refuge for those who searched honestly for the warm comforts of a stable, intelligible moral pattern in their physical environment. The deep need for such order that the devout and logical Anglican Dodgson expressed overtly in his daily affairs and covertly in his imaginative works could, for many, no longer be satisfied by those genial forays into shapely nature and natural history in which so many genteel English amateurs had indulged before Darwin. It might therefore be symbolically important that Dodgson's hobbies were usually ordered not naturally but mechanically—photography, music boxes, mechanical toys, cerebral puzzles and games. In his conscious pastimes at least, Dodgson was wise enough to avoid what his own Cheshire Cat declares unavoidable for the deeply curious—going among mad people—wise enough to avoid journeys to the threatening natural substratum under the brittle surface of his orderly, civilized, conventionally religious existence.

But in Lewis Carroll's truthful literary fantasies, games and toys will not suffice: the ends of his *Alice* games are in many ways arbitrary and forced, the search for the Snark is doomed to failure, the riddle of the Raven and the Writing Desk—that is, the connection between predatory, amoral nature and polite civilization, between nature and the constructed word—has no answer. Except for his adored Alice, his dream creatures symbolize a permanent confusion, not the merely physical, and thus solvable, puzzles of something like Darwin's strange Galápagos Islands creatures. The explanations that Carroll's fantasies seem to call for from within nature are never to be found. There can be no telos, no final goal or ultimate "meaning" within Alice's biological nature or her natural surroundings: her natural curiosity and her human need for what she calls "the meaning of it all" (W, 86) make her, like us, a permanent stranger to her natural environment. She will never attain that Eden she calls "the loveliest garden you ever saw" (W, 10); she can never again secure the unitary womb existence of life before separation, division, and fragmentation; she is now forever an alien, out of the womb, bereft of the cosmic "cradle endlessly rocking," as Walt Whitman put it in the year that Darwin's *Origin* appeared.[2] And the creatures Alice meets will always go round their mad tea tables and pointless caucus rings, with no possible rationale or goal, no stop to their endless circles—graphic metaphors for the Darwinian model of nature's instinctual, endless round of adaptation and self-preservation and of the permanent schism between the workings of nature and the human spirit's need for closure, completeness, and final meaning.

Evil/Live

The fault here lies of course in life itself. When Alice complains to the Cheshire Cat that the croquet game seems to have no rules, she couples this with "and you've no idea how confusing it is all the things being alive" (W, 67). After Darwin, life—"being alive"—becomes almost by definition a maddening moral confusion. The lovable imp Bruno in Carroll's *Sylvie and Bruno Concluded* (1893), seeing the letters EVIL arranged by Sylvie on a board as one of his "lessons" and asked by

Sylvie what they spell, exclaims, "Why it's LIVE, backwards!" The narrator (clearly associated with the author) sympathetically adds in parentheses, "(I thought it was, indeed)." Some Carroll critics cite this passage as a clue to Dodgson's psychology; but they generally miss its direct and crucial relationship to Carroll's "backwards" literary dream fantasies—to the *evil* confusion in all the living things being alive, to the darkness and old chaos inherent in living and dying nature after Darwin's simple biological vision has settled on the world, after innocent, childlike Darwinian curiosity and the need for extrahuman completion and stasis have enticed us "backwards" down the rabbit hole and behind our manufactured anthropomorphic looking-glasses.

Carroll's comedy, then, contributes to the final destruction of a sustaining vision of nature and human nature in orderly harmony, moving steadily and according to divine rules toward some divine end. Such a vision hopefully concludes the chief philosophical poem of the age, Tennyson's *In Memoriam* (1837–50). Tennyson's long elegy ends with a rather forced, hopeful assertion that the human race (along with all natural creation) moves inexorably along a clear path toward a higher state of being and consciousness, where nature will make complete moral sense "like an open book" and where, ultimately, the seemingly mindless, random, amoral multiplicity, and violent waste of "Nature, red in tooth and claw" (*In Memoriam,* section 56, line 15) will attain the coherent singleness of an orderly cosmos lovingly designed for humankind and justly ruled by one God:

> That God, which ever lives and loves,
> One God, one law, one element,
> And one far-off divine event,
> To which the whole creation moves.
> (section 131, lines 141–44)

The natural moral progress, the sense of unitary, purposeful, God-given order and natural motion within an ultimate rest celebrated here by Tennyson (and by Tennyson's stunning music) were by mid-century already a kind of outdated, forced, wishful vision for many intellectuals (and probably for Tennyson himself in his less public roles).[3] And, among other things, the *Alice* books should be understood as representing the completion of this disillusionment—a strangely comical announcement of a new age of dark human consciousness.

Indeed, in *Wonderland* the sort of wishful progressive evolutionism voiced at the end of *In Memoriam* and echoed in much conventional mid- and late-Victorian literature is ridiculed with particular ferocity: for example, a baby can *devolve* into a pig as easily as a pig can *evolve* into a baby. (Darwin's theory, as it was first advanced, made no progressive claims: evolution dealt with adaptive *changes* in species, not with their rise on the hierarchical escalator of moral, spiritual development in some great, God-devised chain of being). In Carroll's comic vision, moreover, motion is mere motion without first cause or final goal. And despite Alice's queening and the implied checkmate at the end of her looking-glass chess game, no one really wins by progressing logically and by deliberately reaching some known and desired end—or everyone wins, as in the pointless caucus race, which in itself nonsensically destroys the very grounds of all teleology. Alice, it is argued in this book, does progress in her Wonderland quest, but only toward a recognition that she must give up that quest and revert to infantile, dependent innocence, denying her frighteningly vivid perceptions of nature's careless, amoral, and unprogressive dance.

ALICE'S EVIDENCE

The final chapter of *Wonderland* is called appropriately "Alice's Evidence," and the subtitle of *Looking-Glass* is "*And What Alice Found There*": both titles underscore the fact that Alice gains the evidence necessary to impel her to end her threatening dreams. A Victorian Anglican with Dodgson's Broad Church (i.e. liberal) views would, whether consciously or unconsciously, naturally associate the title "Alice's Evidence" with William Paley's celebrated *Natural Theology; or, Evidences of the Existence and Attributes of the Deity Collected from the Appearances of Nature* (1802). Paley's work—usually referred to simply as "Paley's Evidences" or "Evidences"—served, early in the nineteenth century, as one of the principal sources for a rational proof of God's existence based on the argument of orderly design in natural phenomena. Among many Victorian intellectuals, Paley's *Evidences* suffered a fatal blow dealt by the mounting "evidences" presented by modern geology and particularly by modern evolutionary theory—indisputable evidences that natural design results from mere "trial and error," the adaptation and "survival of the fittest," rather than from God's efficient and loving plan. Carroll's play on *Paley's Evidences* in "Alice's Evidence" constitutes, like much of his comedy, a small joke with large, indeed cosmic, applications. The fact that Alice is a little girl operating with the laughable logic of a normal naive child and that Paley was a very grown-up cleric operating with the formidable, but finally laughable, logic of a brilliant adult theologian adds telling irony to the jest.

In order to survive, Alice—like the hyperorderly Charles Dodgson—must create a meaningfully ordered, word-dependent game world out of the morally unintelligible void, and often in opposition to clear evidence from the nature of which we humans are an inseparable part. It could be said that such order is made in spite; and the spiteful element in Dodgson's rejections of disorder (like his clearly spiteful, outspoken rejections of babies and little boys because of their natural messiness) remains never far from the surface of his *Alice* fantasies. Alice's own spitefulness ("Who cares for *you*. . . . You're nothing but a pack of cards!" [*W*, 97], for example) is one of Carroll's means to make her characterization believably human. It also helps explain why modern readers frequently admire what they see as her heroism. Like many spiteful heroines and heroes of failed causes in stage tragedies, Alice is a not altogether attractive figure. But we still admire, even cherish her as our courageous surrogate because she unwittingly learns to act heroically when she fails to find the order she seeks in the surrounding natural chaos. She thus becomes for many modern readers what she undoubtedly was for Dodgson: a naive champion of the doomed human quest for ultimate meaning and lost Edenic order. In the *Alices*, as in twentieth-century existential thought, human meaning is made in spite of the void, and, in making her order and meaning out of, essentially, *nothing*, the brave child Alice spitefully makes—for herself and for us, her elders and her successors—what we might very well call sense out of non-sense, something out of nothing. Ironically, like the nihilistic villain Edmund who declares near the end of *King Lear*, "Some good I mean to do, / Despite of mine own nature," Alice, in resisting her instinctive fears and the moral nothingness of her adventures, somehow makes of her spitefulness an affirmation of the human spirit.

But this is not to say that the *Alice* books are little *King Lears*. For all their tragic implications, they are of course basically, overwhelmingly comic. Accordingly, their heroine, besides persevering and fighting back, has the practical good sense of a comic, rather than a tragic, figure. At the end of each book, she has the good sense to do another necessary human thing, to run away, suppressing the reality of her own true dream-visions and substituting for that reality the comfortable dreams of her above-ground world's waking state.

In any case, Alice's imposed order becomes all the more admirable and precious because of its fragility (the way the *Alice* books have become the cherished, sometimes sacrosanct, possession of deeply troubled adults). The comic tone at the end of *Wonderland*, for example, like the customary tone of Carroll's adult narrator, is so sure of itself because it is ultimately so unsure of itself, because it is forged in shaky anxiety, emerging suddenly and full-blown from the rejection of an orderly person's nightmare of complete disorder. Like the total rejection of any bad dream we have just broken off, Carroll's concluding pages seem to deny completely the validity of adventures that have all the luminosity of our truest experiences, whose creatures and insanities will continue to live indefinitely, we sense, after we reject them and wake to our fragile daydreams of cosmic order. Therefore, the endings of both *Alice* books, contrived and sentimental as they might be, are paradoxically appropriate and true to our ordinary ambiguous experience. Brazen (and frightened) Alice rejects all her evidence as nonsense and dream; chaos and old night are ironically dispelled by mere teatime and a little kitty cat (both fine and delicate symbols of insouciant high civilization); and the final narratives, palpably artificial constructions though they be, seem to explain away sensibly whatever residual conviction of the dream adventures' relevance and validity might persist—in dreamers, readers, or writers whose waking moments are shaped by and dedicated to humanly constructed order.

THE SEARCH FOR ORDER

Lewis Carroll was of course by no means alone in this preoccupation with lost visions of cosmic order and the ache for comforting stasis. These concerns are central to Victorian thought. Framed by Thomas Carlyle at the beginning and Thomas Hardy at the end, Victorian literature offers a comprehensive panorama of intellectual, emotional, and aesthetic responses to the sense of loss and ultimate anarchy discussed here. Carlyle (especially in *Sartor Resartus* [1830–34], arguably the single most influential work of literature in its time) attempts, with some success, to rant and rave himself and his spiritually bereft audience into a new conviction of transcendent order immanent in nature, of a permanent, divine design within the seemingly mindless, mechanical, amoral welter of a new, rapidly changing, industrialized capitalist society and a new scientized Creation from which the old God has disappeared. In a deliberately different key, Hardy writes a postscript to the era in his poem "The Darkling Thrush" (pointedly signed "December 31, 1900"), a cynical representation of the vain human search for permanent coherence, poignantly and ironically underscored by a simple natural image, an aged thrush (like an aged English Romantic poet, a Tennysonian nightingale) singing in pointless, isolated joy, flinging "his soul / Upon the growing gloom." For Hardy, as for a great many of his contemporaries, the earlier, rather desperate Victorian search for a meaningful moral pattern within nature ("terrestrial things") had failed abysmally. For him, his age culminated in the spirit of his final stanza:

So little cause for carolings
Of such ecstatic sound
Was written on terrestrial things
Afar or nigh around,
That I could think there trembled through
His happy good-night air
Some blessed Hope, whereof he knew
And I was unaware.[4]

But in the middle of the period, Lewis Carroll represents something different. His comic fantasies of the mid-1860s and early 1870s stand in curious contrast to the attitudes toward ultimate order found in most major Victorian literary texts. And on this contrast rests, perhaps, Carroll's strongest claim to a place in the construction of modernism. The order that is restored at the ends of both *Alices* is no typical "Victorian compromise" between a horror vision of nature's moral disorder and a consoling assertion of some traditional moral order within nature. Missing in Carroll is even that nostalgic sadness, that vain longing, that hopeless but "blessed Hope" Hardy half senses in darkening nature, a spirit that might revive some corresponding, if ephemeral, hope in us. Instead, Carroll's final above-ground order stands fully isolated, discontinuous from the literal anarchy of Alice's adventures and the metaphysical and moral anarchy they represent. Instead of compromise, here at the ends of both *Alice* books (especially *Wonderland*) is a defiant, spiteful, total, and uncompromising rejection of one vision and a complacent, comic reassertion of another— one, significantly, that no longer appears to retain a shred of philosophical validity, even within its own field of play, the adventures themselves.

Like a haughty member of the upper classes staring down an incontrovertible but class-threatening fact, like a colonial official maintaining an ideologically constructed order against actual rebellion in some God-forsaken outpost of European imperialism and "civilization," the frame story of each *Alice* book stands in direct, defiant opposition to the body of the book, the vivid adventures themselves. When Humpty Dumpty tells Alice, "the question is . . . which is to be master—that's all" (*L,* 163), his assertion—like Alice's early declaration that the "great puzzle" is "Who in the world am I?" (*W,* 15)—has profound existential, linguistic, political, social, and economic significance. He is master of his world because he *chooses* to believe he is in spite of the actual circumstances and because in his class-ordered, hierarchical, money-driven world, he has the power (words and money and force) and the elevated position (class and proper diction) to pay for and command obedience—and thus a kind of existence and order. Who "in the world" we are (and who we are "in the world") is a function of how we order (master, boss about, bully, verbalize, and force into a coherent order) our essentially unorderable worlds. Never mind that the ideological grounds, the "natural" justification for our mastery over members of lower classes and conquered peoples or over the intransigent moral chaos underlying all classes and systems are, after Darwin and the disappearance of God, as fragile as Humpty Dumpty's eggshell and as precarious as his perch. At the end of her *Looking-Glass* adventures, Alice says of their "dreadful confusion," "I can't stand this any longer!" (*L,* 204). Similarly, at the end of her *Wonderland* adventures she finally decides she will have no more of their even more dreadful confusion. Like Humpty Dumpty, she decides for herself what to call this dreaded and uncontrollable chaos—and she calls it a "curious dream," mere "nonsense" (sense though it most certainly appears to be). So too do the ends of both fantasies define as "wonderful" and "nonsense" what we and Alice have just experienced vividly as frightening reality, asserting through their structure as well as their content that they too will have none of it. For at this point in the adventures and the narratives there appears no sane choice for humans but to seize power, to impose the fragile, artificial, arbitrary order of above-ground human law, culture, and social convention, using their shaky words and signs as the primary means of mastery.

Of course, like the White Knight, who says of his silly upside-down box "it's my own invention," we sometimes allow ourselves to recognize that such order and such power are merely our own silly, upside-down inventions of a world made whole. But generally we keep up our guard, and such chilling recognitions come to us only indirectly and even then artfully disguised in oblique fantasies, jokes, nonsense, games, and dreams—not straight and not in that uncensored daylight we choose to call sober, unadorned everyday life. Besides, we are also well aware at some level of comprehension of the final danger: if our eggshell, invented, but coherent waking world really fell and shattered, we too, like the imperious but fragile Humpty Dumpty, could never be put together again.

Thus, like the aesthetic order of much modern art, like Matthew Arnold's "culture" in the face of impending "anarchy," the final order of the *Alice* books is not an order discovered in objective nature, but an order openly imposed on nature—a human meaning and coherence that frames and shapes a morally shapeless void. Like Wallace Stevens's singer whose song "mastered the night and portioned out the sea," Alice, with her naive declaration that all the assembled disorderly creatures of her disorganized adventures are "nothing but a pack of cards," masters them with restrictive language in order to satisfy what Stevens calls our "blessed rage . . . to order the words . . . of ourselves and of our origins."[5] Like Stevens's plain and shapely jar, simply "placed" in the wild nature of Tennessee, Alice's simple final declarations make the forever "slovenly wilderness" of her underground adventures in raw Darwinian nature take on *her* order, shape, and meaning. Like Stevens's jar, her childish declarations of mastery take dominion not only over her particular nightmares of chaos, but also, in a sense, as Stevens puts it, "dominion everywhere."[6] And this, for many of Carroll's modern readers, makes the *Alice* books especially precious. The question is not whether Alice's ordering of night and sea, of herself and her origins, is ultimately valid in terms of physical nature as we post-Darwinians know it. The question is much more pressing and pragmatic: it is whether Alice is capable of fulfilling her human potential *despite* her own nature and that nature of which she must remain a permanent part.

Joseph Conrad's *Heart of Darkness* (1899), a crucial document in the development of modernism, gives us the frame story of Marlow, a very pragmatic, simple, rather literal-minded and naive young man who abhors lying, but who finally lies to preserve a necessary illusion that gives life some moral order and significance. Rather than tell a dead idealist's naive fiancée that her dying imperialist lover's last words as he looked into the very heart of darkness that lay around him deep in the Belgian Congo as well as within his own depraved nature and the brutal "civilizing" acts of his culture were "The horror! The horror!" Marlow tells this innocent what he thinks she needs to hear: "The last word he pronounced," says Marlow, "was—your name." For, as Marlow says, to tell her the truth he had learned in his surrealistic, underground adventures, to destroy her groundless faith—"that great and saving illusion that shone with an unearthly glow . . . in the triumphant darkness"—would have made their present world "too dark—too dark altogether."[7] Similarly, for Alice (or Dodgson or Lewis Carroll) to call her horrible dreams of dark chaos actual "chaos" would be too horrible, too dark altogether. So she (along with her creator) ends these journeys into her own heart of darkness (and ours) by assigning them pleasurable names, by sunnily telling herself (and us) that they were "wonderful," nice, nonsensical dreams populated by silly playing cards, funny chessmen, and pointless players of pointless games.

ALICE AS ARTIST

Moreover, because she is child, dreamer, liar, and namegiver, Alice is also, in many ways, artist—a player of very special games.[8] And like many modern artists, she moves toward creating an ominous, rather illusory beauty and order out of dangerous, disorderly, and essentially ugly and grotesque materials—not by denying the existence of these materials, but rather by shaping them into what she (and we) can call patterned, plotted "adventures," through her human, blessed rage for order.

In a sense, then, Carroll's naive child-heroine prefigures the central spirit behind the twentieth-century dependence on art as an essential, if fragile, source for those transcendent visions of coherence that are necessary to make human existence bearable. Wallace Stevens's unnamed singer in the heart of darkness at Key West—at the tip, that is, of a fragile civilization, a final dot in a vast dark sea—sings "among / The meaningless plungings of water and the wind." She could easily be a direct descendant of Carroll's Alice. Her attractiveness to Stevens's adult speaker standing in the darkness is like the appeal of the innocent child Alice Liddell to the experienced, order worshiper Charles Dodgson—and the appeal of the *Alice* books to a modern reader:

> It was her voice that made
> The sky acutest at its vanishing.
> She measured to the hour its solitude.
> She was the single artificer of the world
> In which she sang. And when she sang, the sea,
> Whatever self it had, became the self
> That was her song, for she was the maker.
>
> Then we,
> As we beheld her striding there alone,
> Knew that there never was a world for her
> Except the one she sang and, singing, made.
> (Stevens, 129–30, lines 34–43)

A naive forerunner of the modern artist-hero figure, Alice resists succumbing to the despair provoked by her perceptions of absurdity. Instead of drowning in her own tears (a primal salt sea filled with the life of all those Darwinian natural creatures—and with a carefully drawn ape significantly in the center of Dodgson's original *under Ground* illustration [see Figure 1]), she leads the way to that fantastical shore where games can still be played and tales told. Along with her fastidious creator, Alice persists, despite many daunting setbacks, and finally seems to win the game for us all.

Thus, in his comic approach to the modern problem of finding new metaphysical order in an intellectual environment hostile to such order, hostile even to the search itself, Lewis Carroll ushers in our age. His *Alice*s prefigure the voyage on which many contemporary men

Figure 1. The Pool of Tears in *Alice's Adventures under Ground.*

and women now find themselves—a voyage into their own hearts of darkness, without the old maps, without even a reasonable hope of replacing them. This is the voyage begun so casually by curious Alice in her *Adventures under Ground* and extended in its fascinating sequels—*Alice in Wonderland, Through the Looking-Glass,* and *The Hunting of the Snark.*

Florence Becker Lennon has written, "It is because Lewis Carroll sensed the irrationalities, the under side of the carpet, the lions behind the staircase—the beast in man and the indifference of the universe— that he was a great poet. He was able to deal with contradictions and horrors and irrationalities, and to convert them into an art form that gives release to children and adults alike."[9] This release through art— this delicate comic shaping and celebration of the permanent paradoxes of the human condition—is one reason today's adult readers around the world cherish their Lewis Carroll more than ever, thankful that he accompanies them on their necessary quest for their meaning and order.

7

Laughing and Grief:
What's So Funny about the *Alices*?*

Nothing is funnier than unhappiness.
—Nell, in Samuel Beckett's *Endgame*

By now, readers might well be objecting that the interpretations in this book hardly square with their own impressions of the comic ambience of the *Alice* books—a lighthearted spirit that often provokes simple open laughter, rather than the fear and convoluted existential angst I have suggested in *Wonderland* or the sober reflections on human development I have outlined in *Through the Looking-Glass*. In fact, one answer to the question posed at the beginning of this book, one reason for the curiously widespread, enduring admiration of the *Alices* is, surely, the easy accessibilty of their elementary comedy. Addressed initially to a very young audience and chosen with Carroll's characteristic authorial fastidiousness and deep respect for children's sensibilities, much of the direct humor, many of the simple jokes couched in simple diction can survive translation, shifts in cultural discourse, and the passage of time with an ease denied to works that depend for their effects on such devices as subtle word play or complex satirical allusions to adult, historically specific topics.

*This chapter is based on "Laughing and Grief: What's So Funny about *Alice in Wonderland?*" in *Lewis Carroll Observed,* ed. Edward Guiliano (New York: Clarkson Potter, 1976), 1–18.

Laughing and Grief

Obviously, any interpretation of the *Alices* must recognize that the books are indeed funny and that much of their popular and critical success comes from the distinct quality of their comedy. But the issue is not as simple as it might seem. For the dark and serious undersides of Alice's adventures—the threatening, epistemologically subversive elements on which the interpretations in this book have concentrated—*do* continually show through the books' surface textures of plain fun and games. The ominous aptness of Carroll's original title remains, like the vanishing smile of his Cheshire Cat, a powerful presence, only partially veiled by his substitution of "wonder" for "under" and "land" for "ground." And the dangers as well as rewards of seeing "through" our fragile, constructed looking-glasses, the revealing illuminations in what we, like Alice, "find there" on the other side are as often matters for sober reflection as for carefree amusement.

So in the search for their meaning and their sources of enduring power, we here encounter yet another curiosity about the *Alices*, another set of critical questions: How is it that so many readers remember them as playful, sunny books of uncomplicated laughter when they are laced with disturbing ontological complexities and recount some of the most terrifying adventures in modern literature? How can we explain the fact that the *Alices* are laughable when at the same time they pose insoluble problems of existence and dramatize a frightful descent into sheer madness, when they are heavily punctuated with Alice's tears and expressions of despair, when her final reactions to the "dreadful confusion" (*L,* 204) of the adventures include in one book a "scream, half of fright and half of anger" (*W,* 97) and in the other the heartfelt cry, "I can't stand this any longer!" (*L,* 204)?

Considering that the *Alice* books address many of the deepest, most disturbing questions that perplex the modern mind and that they are full of frightening, macabre scenes and characters, how in the world do they manage simultaneously to be so funny? What is the substance of their peculiar ("Carrollian") comedy, and how does that comedy help to shape their central insights and their effects upon adult readers? The answers to these questions involve two distinct yet interdependent issues. First, simply, what makes the *Alice* books comic?

That is, what incidents, characters, details, and strategies within their observable surfaces (as well as what satirical targets outside) create their comedy? Second, and not so simply, why *must* the *Alices* be comic works? This question is concerned primarily with the books' metaphysical and psychological dynamics: their need to be funny and our need to find them so.

The widespread tendency among critics to lump both *Alices* together indiscriminately, despite all their obvious differences in subject matter, style, and tone, has generally prevented satisfying answers to such questions. For the two books differ sharply in the nature of their comedy. Successful as the comedy of *Through the Looking-Glass* is, it still seems, when compared with the comedy of *Wonderland*, rather forced and regimented, predetermined by the book's "backwards" field of play and the rules of its game—a product more of its author's mirroring intellect and strong will than of the liberated, playful imagination that created (by a process akin to the free association of daydreaming) *Alice's Adventures under Ground* some seven or eight years earlier when the younger Dodgson allowed his mind to leap with his child-heroine into an absurd underworld with no notion of "where in the world" (or outside it) the leap would carry them. In fact, *Through the Looking-Glass* might well be understood in this context as Dodgson's deliberate but failed attempt to recapture the delicate, spontaneous comic spirit of *Wonderland*. However, there were compensations for this failure. As Harry Levin has remarked, *Through the Looking-Glass* "made up in systematic elaboration for what it lost in spontaneous flow."[1] So, too, its comedy made up in orderliness, focus, and applicability for what it lost in free exuberance and unself-conscious play.

Because understanding the nature and function of the comedy in *Alice's Adventures in Wonderland* is, then, a much trickier task than it is in the case of *Through the Looking-Glass*, this discussion will concentrate on *Wonderland*, leaving for the reader the easier question of the comic dynamics in *Through the Looking-Glass*. But what follows applies in some important ways to both books.

The first question—What readily observable elements make for

Wonderland's comedy?—has been dealt with thoroughly in the past 70 years by competent scholars and critics. Perceptive critical studies of the *Alices* like those by William Empson and Harry Morgan Ayres[2] and annotated editions like those by Martin Gardner, Peter Heath, and James Kincaid[3] have demonstrated how witty and subtle is Carroll's oblique satire of Victorian thought, custom, and morality. Nevertheless, unprofessional readers can usually do quite well themselves here without the aid of critics and annotated editions—a fact that in itself reveals an important aspect of Carroll's comedy. For despite the scattered satirical references to clearly topical matters such as mid-Victorian manners and politics, Darwinian theory, or particular nineteenth-century children's books and poems,[4] and some rather incidental references to unfamiliar mathematical and logical principles,[5] the comedy of the *Alices* refers by and large to matters of common knowledge: adult readers today can, unaided, recognize the overt elements that continue to make *Alice's Adventures in Wonderland* comic. For example, the chief targets of its richest satire—the pompous and unwarranted assumptions and stances of the adult world (so often aped by children) represented by its wonderful collection of ridiculous, self-assured character types—are immediately comprehensible and funny to adult readers.

CHILDREN'S NEGATIVE REACTIONS

Although the objects of Carroll's comedy are plain, the operative principles of his comic process still require explication. An investigation of those principles might best begin by recognizing an important empirical fact: many children fail to find *Wonderland* amusing. This is not because the book's comic references, like youth, are wasted on the young, although the fact that children do not catch all of the best jokes and probably catch too little of the narrator's humorous, avuncular tone is a part of the issue. Children are put off by Alice's underground adventures not because they cannot understand them; in fact, they frequently understand them too well. Indeed, they often find the book a terrifying experience (as innumerable undergraduates have reported to me over the years), rarely relieved by the comic spirit they can clearly perceive. Katherine Anne Porter's reaction is fairly typical of published accounts of this phenomenon. As a child, she reports, she "believed in it entirely. The difference between it and the other fairy stories is that all this takes place in a setting of everyday life. The little glass table with the key on it, and the furniture and the gardens and the flowers they were all things we knew, you see, familiar things dreadfully out of place, and they frightened me."[6]

Just below the surface of these threatening, strangely realistic adventures lurk all sorts of even more threatening psychological implications, easily identified and cataloged by readers with the merest smattering of Freud. As William Empson told I. A. Richards, "There are things in *Alice* that would give Freud the creeps."[7] Child readers most certainly sense those creepy things; and if they would give the terribly adult and analytical Dr. Freud the creeps, imagine what they might do to poor innocents unequipped for sorting such things out into safe, comfortable, rather dull analytic categories. Indeed, Paul Schilder, an eminent American psychiatrist of the 1930s, believed the unconscious, primitive material in the *Alice* books to be so threatening to children's psyches that he urged, in a notorious 1937 address to the American Psychoanalytic Society, that children be forbidden to read them![8]

Significantly, the same out-of-place, familiar details of *Alice in Wonderland* that frighten children tend to have the reverse effect on adults: what confuses and frequently repels children amuses and attracts adults. What is it, then, about *Alice's Adventures in Wonderland* that makes it *simultaneously* a dangerously regressive, primal horror experience for one audience but a comic delight for the other? Freud's theories of jokes and the unconscious can provide some help with this question,[9] but the whole answer cannot, need not, be found there.

Often we find "poor Alice" (one of the narrator's favorite epithets) crying over what we—and the narrator—find amusing. In fact (and adult readers tend to forget this), the times Alice cries or otherwise displays her apprehensions, fears, and despair greatly outnumber those times she displays any emotion one could conceivably count as pleasure or joy. True, once during her nightmarish adventures she cannot "help bursting out laughing" (*W*, 66); but this atypical reaction (here to the hedgehog-turned-croquet-ball) can also be attributed to her nervousness, her anxiety over Wonderland's devastating reversals of such above-ground certainties as the distinctions between animate and inanimate existence. For Alice, as for most seven-year-olds, Wonderland's confusing breakdown of the "rules" and of the premises of her sense of order is no laughing matter; lying at its center (as it lies at the center of her adventures in "The Mad Tea-Party" chapter) is anarchy and total madness. And even when the dangerous absurdity of Wonderland might tempt Alice to a bit of nervous laughter, the gravity of all the mad creatures (they never laugh or display amusement, not even the smiling Cheshire Cat—another characteristic that can make them funny for adults but scary for young children) indicates the proper attitude for a polite and frightened Victorian child. For example, in awarding the silly prizes after the pointless caucus race, "Alice thought the whole thing very absurd, but they all looked so grave that she did not dare to laugh; as she could not think of anything to say, she simply bowed, and took the thimble, looking as solemn as she could" (*W*, 24). Not really a completely amusing situation for Alice (or for the child readers who might naturally identify with her), however funny it might be for adults.

CHILD VS. ADULT SYMPATHIES

Keeping in mind, then, those child readers and their disturbing identification with the confused, threatened, and frightened Alice, and those adult readers who, at their most conscious levels of apprehension, would identify with the calm, unconfused, obviously adult narrator, let us consider more closely several other passages from the text.

Take, first, Alice's early, terrifying problems with her unpredictable, bizarre changes of size and the surreal situation in chapter 4 when she grows too large for the womblike space in which she is confined (a scene that occasioned one of Carroll's eeriest illustrations for his *under Ground* manuscript [see Figure 2]). These fearful changes and Alice's understandably anxious reactions to them begin early; thus, in chapter 2, we read:

> Poor Alice! It was as much as she could do, lying down on one side, to look through into the garden with one eye; but to get through was more hopeless than ever: she sat down and began to cry again.
>   "You ought to be ashamed of yourself," said Alice, "a great girl like you," (she might well say this), "to go on crying in this way!" (*W*, 15)

The narrator's little joke here on poor Alice's horrible size—"she might well say," " 'a great girl like you' "—illustrates an important component of the book's comic strategy. The fact that this comic intrusion, slipped in by the adult narrator, is, like several others, pointedly parenthetical (coming, so to speak, right in the middle of Alice's painful thoughts) symbolizes graphically the close yet delicately distanced relationships between adult and child, narrator and Alice, pleasure and pain, comedy and horror that throughout characterize the distinctive, complex comedy of *Wonderland*.

This gently joking little parenthetical remark mirrors the dominant surface texture of the entire book: although the narrator soon stops making such intrusive jokes and returns to them only at the end of the adventures, he remains constantly present through the agency of a distinctly adult attitude and tone. That attitude and tone—lucid, calm, reassuring, faintly amused, rather snobbish, loving, and indulgent but often a bit distant and sometimes even slightly hostile—pulls deftly but forcefully against the fantastic, threatening, even horrible events it narrates, creating a precarious balance between the two major opposing forces that energize the adventures.

When the final, Kafkaesque trial begins, the narrator intrudes again:

> Alice had never been in a court of justice before, but she had read about them in books, and she was quite pleased to find that she

(A)

(B)

Figure 2. Alice (A) in the Rabbit's house in *Alice's Adventures under Ground,* chapter 2, and (B) in *Alice's Adventures in Wonderland,* chapter 4.

knew the name of nearly everything there. "That's the judge," she said to herself, "because of his great wig."

The judge, by the way, was the King; and, as he wore his crown over the wig (look at the frontispiece if you want to see how he did it), he did not look at all comfortable, and it was certainly not becoming.

"And that's the jury-box," thought Alice; "and those twelve creatures," (she was obliged to say "creatures," you see, because some of them were animals, and some were birds), "I suppose they are the jurors." She said this last word two or three times over to herself, being rather proud of it: for she thought, and rightly too, that very few little girls of her age knew the meaning of it at all. (W, 86)

This self-assured witticism of the narrator—his "and rightly too," which gently, even lovingly perhaps, ridicules Alice who thinks that because she knows the names she knows the "meaning" of it all, but instead knows nothing of the meaning—invites the adult reader into complicity with the semiotically sophisticated narrator: both experienced adults laugh at and at the same time sympathize with the naive child Alice.

The adventures include a number of episodes that depend more on physical circumstances than on verbal wit to generate a similar comic tension between the detached amusement of an adult observer and the terrified engagement of the child participant. There is, for example, the episode in which poor Alice almost drowns in her own tears—a little joke for adults perhaps (a typical Carrollian hypostatic conversion, a verbal hyperbole comically exaggerated by being taken suddenly, in dreams, as literal and given concrete dramatic form), but surely no joke for those many child readers who have yet to learn thoroughly that many idiomatic expressions like "drowning in one's tears" are merely verbal constructions. And certainly no joke for poor Alice, who is, as a matter of fact, throughout *Wonderland* threatened with violent death—by falling, drowning, going out like a spent candle, being trapped in a womblike space too small for her rapidly growing body, and decapitation.

These brief glances at the text reveal several sorts of wit and humor operating at once and merging into that peculiar *Wonderland* comedy critics sometimes lazily sum up with casual, catchall terms like "Carrollian nonsense." The complacent adult in each adult reader smiles and laughs with the adult narrator, and yet (like that narrator) also sympathizes with "poor Alice's" consternation and fear. Why? Not simply because all adults were once children, but because a part of us all remains forever the child, because in our deepest fantasies and as the dreamers of our most vivid dreams we too are often frightened children, unsure of and yet yearning to trust all the constructed grounds of our more or less orderly universe. Our wakeful facade self of rational, self-assured, sophisticated adulthood, meager and fragile as it is, must not permit us a full apperception of its meagerness and fragility. It must, among other things, employ laughter to censor and dispel our own worst (and best) insights and fears. Censor and dispel them, by all means, but also, simultaneously, allow them concrete dramatic expression—an ambiguous trick of the mind, which so fascinated Freud and his followers.[10]

ENTERING THE CHILD'S MIND

Carroll's particular comic genius therefore depends heavily on his uncanny ability to enter fully the mind of childhood, to become the child who dreams our adult dreams. This ability is celebrated by many admirers of the *Alice* books. Virginia Woolf goes even further, understanding Carroll as a fortunate case of what might be called arrested development. "Childhood," she writes,

> normally fades slowly. Wisps of childhood persist when the boy or girl is a grown man or woman. Childhood returns sometimes by day, more often by night. But it was not so with Lewis Carroll. For some reason, we know not what, his childhood was sharply severed. It lodged in him whole and entire. . . . [H]e could do what no one else has ever been able to do—he could return to that world; he could re-create it, so that we too become children again. . . . It is for

this reason that the two Alices are not books for children; they are the only books in which we become children.[11]

Despite her perceptiveness here, Woolf pushes the insight too far, neglecting Carroll's clearly adult, experienced narrator who serves as the mature reader's surrogate and whose ever-present, consistently humorous voice provides throughout a countervailing comic force. The powerful tensions that *Alice's Adventures in Wonderland* establishes between these two poles—the reader as amused adult and that adult reader as frightened child—create in their complex oppositions and interpenetrations an internal comic drama that plays with the most fundamental incongruities of human existence, ones that reside, paradoxically separate and yet fused, in each adult reader's psyche.

The child in many of us will be frightened and repelled by Alice's adventures and yet (a bit like the curious, daring Alice herself) will often be attracted, too. However, a large part of that inner child's motivating force, like a very large part of Alice's, wants escape. Carroll's underground world of quite probable absurdities is not at all funny to that portion of our selves. While Wonderland offers a refreshing respite, a play area secure from all the constrictions and confinements of time, space, size, logic, manners, social class—all constructed above-ground order—at the same time it dramatically reveals the ultimate threat to our fragile psychological and metaphysical identities and our orderly, albeit synthethic, perception of our universe. Alice's escape at the end, effected by naming her very real subterranean experiences mere "nonsense," is certainly a comic conclusion. But it is surely not the final resolution, the definitive escape from misadventures we enjoy in most traditional comedies. Indeed, like the narrator's attitude all along, Alice's swift escape-by-naming has some whistling in the dark about it.

MISREMEMBERING

Thus, while Alice's last thoughts are of the "wonderful dream" from which she has just awakened, one senses an unwitting irony in her choice of the word "wonderful." Nevertheless, for Alice, as for most dreamers, many of the worst dreams must be remembered—or, more accurately, *mis*remembered—as our best, our most "wonderful" dreams, just as the necessarily sinister elements in the best jokes must remain submerged if the jokes are to work.

Apparently, 4 July 1862—the day Dodgson claimed to have composed the original "under Ground" stories orally and extemporaneously for Alice Liddell and her sisters—was not, as he wrote some 25 years later, a "golden afternoon," a "slumberous scene" under a "cloudless blue above."[12] It was, according to the Meteorological Office's weather record, "cool and wet." Nevertheless, like the warm golden patina that gilds the popular memory of the *Alice* books and the genial comic spirit that suffuses them (mainly through the agency of the narrative voice), Dodgson's often repeated description of the occasion has become a permanent part of the *Alice* legend and somehow enhances the book's comic effect. The opening words of *Wonderland,* the prefatory poem (added in Carroll's 1865 published expansion of the original 1862–63 *under Ground* manuscript) already incorporates the meteorological fiction, starting readers off with the sunny, unthreatening line, "All in the golden afternoon" (*W,* 3). The poetic license Carroll takes here in renaming the actual weather is similar to the creative license we sometimes take with our most uncomical, but perhaps truest dreams, immediately reconstructing and then remembering them soon afterwards as funny nonsense. In the comic spirit of that (mis)remembering and naming we frequently forge our sanity.

Many children, incapable of viewing Alice's adventures entirely as someone else's dreams, no doubt appreciate the last pages of the books best and never ask grown-ups for the stories again. Grown-ups, on the other hand, have returned enthusiastically over and over to those adventures, making the *Alice*s two of the most quoted, revered books in our language. These adults return to Alice's adventures because, like their original dreamer, they have at one mental stratum been able to distance themselves from the adventures' threatening personal implications, categorizing the most ominous episodes as "nonsense," naming them as someone else's comic dream fragments that bear no immediate referential significance. With the urbane and detached narrator as their familiar guide and alter ego, adult readers can enter, share, suffer, laugh at, and then leave the crazy dream worlds of the *Alices* protected from their full destructive implications. One of Carroll's great achievements in these books is the creation of the means for readers to experience Alice's dreams exactly as if they were their own dreams, dramatizations of their own deep-seated desires and anxieties, at the same time that he makes that experience comic—finally therapeutic rather than destructive.

Laughter, we should remind ourselves, is by no means reserved for optimistic, sunny views of the world. Nineteenth- and twentieth-century literature in particular offers many splendid examples of works that, in their explorations of the absurd human condition, incite *both* terror and joy, sorrow and laughter. Thus, the horror comedy suggested here is by no means unfamiliar to us, nor was it unfamiliar to many of Carroll's original Victorian readers. One can find numerous variations of this comedy. Jonathan Swift comes immediately to mind.[13] The Fool's speeches in *King Lear* or the fantasy of some metaphysical poems are not so different from the macabre humor of *Alice in Wonderland*. Surely, a number of Dickens's novels qualify here. The twentieth-century stage abounds in dramas like the absurdist *Waiting for Godot* and *Endgame,* which are at once fantastic, realistic, hilarious, frightening, and abjectly pessimistic. Recent "black" humorists and "sick" comedians created a whole body of comic work based on grim underground visions of the absurd human condition. Even one of the grimmest of the moderns, Kafka (the author perhaps most often invoked in contemporary Carroll criticism), considered himself a comic writer, a writer whose most ghastly and horrifying works actually provoked among his first readers frequent and full laughter.[14]

HORRIFIC ILLUSTRATIONS

Carroll was not completely unaware of the sort of "impure" comedy he was producing, despite some of his disclaimers. His original illustrations for *Alice's Adventures under Ground* demonstrate that at some imaginative level he certainly sensed the horrific elements of that comedy. Most readers picture only Tenniel's illustrations when they summon up concrete visual images of the *Alice* books. Those delightful illustrations have become so integral a part of the institutionalized literary experience we call "Alice" that Tenniel's renditions of the adventures constitute for most people the "official" ones; the ones that shape their perceptions of the verbal texts. Carroll's drawings, however—naive and primitive as they might seem—often better illustrate both the original and the published book. They do so mainly because they better reflect the horror comedy that pervades both texts.[15] Tenniel's illustrations, excellent as they are, might well be considered in this context a kind of sugaring over of Carroll's threatening implications, the way daytime reconstructions of nightmares tend to repress the nightmares' worst episodes and most disturbing revelations. Like the shift in titles from "under Ground" to the relatively innocuous "Wonderland," or the creation of a "golden" sunny afternoon from a "cool and wet" one, this shift from Carroll's often horrifying illustrations to Tenniel's rather comfortable ones fails, however, to dispel completely the permanent horrors that reside in the substance of Carroll's comic fantasy.

A few illustrations should demonstrate my point. Figure 3 juxtaposes the *under Ground* Queen of Hearts with the *Wonderland* King and Queen of Hearts. Carroll's drawing (the final drawing in the *under Ground* manuscript) possesses an eerie, disquieting, kinetic power missing from the relatively tame, gentle, frozen, and contained comedy of Tenniel's rendition. Although Carroll was obviously not an accomplished draftsman and Tenniel was one of the most famous cartoonists of his day, Carroll's illustration gains in intensity from its intimate physical relationship to its text; Tenniel's, on the other hand, stands in a formally separated relation to the text (as do all of Tenniel's other illustrations in the first edition). Carroll's pictures, like William Blake's illuminations for his poems, often grow out of the adventures; Tenniel's tend to illustrate them in relatively static designs. The same intimate relationship and the same eerie, active threats (especially threatening for a child reader) are observed in the Figure 4 drawing, which communicates Alice's real misery.

(A)

(B)

Figure 3. (A) Carroll's Queen of Hearts in *Alice's Adventures under Ground,* chapter 4, and (B) Tenniel's King and Queen of Hearts in *Alice's Adventures in Wonderland,* chapter 8.

for she could not remember having ever seen one. However, nothing more happened, so she decided on going into the garden at once, but, alas for poor Alice! when she got to the door, she found she had forgotten the little golden key, and when she went back to the table for the key, she found she could not possibly reach it. she could see it plainly enough through the glass, and she tried her best to climb up one of the legs of the table, but it was too slippery, and when she had tired herself out with trying, the poor little thing sat down and cried.

"Come! there's no use in crying!" said Alice to herself rather sharply, "I advise you to leave off this minute." (she generally gave herself very good advice, and sometimes scolded herself so severely as to bring tears into her eyes, and once she remembered boxing her own ears for having been unkind to herself

Figure 4. Carroll's illustration for *Alice's Adventures under Ground*, chapter 1.

119

(A)   (B)

Figure 5. (A) Carroll's illustrations for chapters 1 and 3 in *Alice's Adventures under Ground* and (B) Tenniel's illustration for chapter 2 in *Alice's Adventures in Wonderland*.

This time Alice waited quietly until it chose to speak again: in a few minutes the caterpillar took the hookah out of its mouth, and got down off the mushroom, and crawled away into the grass, merely remarking as it went: "the top will make you grow taller, and the stalk will make you grow shorter."

"The top of <u>what</u>? the stalk of <u>what</u>!" thought Alice.

"Of the mushroom," said the caterpillar, just as if she had asked it aloud, and in another moment it was out of sight.

Alice remained looking thoughtfully at the mushroom for a minute, and then picked it and carefully broke it in two, taking the stalk in one hand, and the top in the other. "<u>Which</u> does the stalk do?" she said, and nibbled a little bit of it to try: the next mo-ment she felt a violent blow on her chin: it had struck her foot!

Figure 6. Carroll's illustration for *Alice's Adventures under Ground*, chapter 3.

(A)

(B)

Figure 7. (A) Carroll's illustration of the Gryphon and Mock Turtle in *Alice's Adventures under Ground,* chapter 4, and (B) Tenniel's illustrations of the Gryphon and Mock Turtle in *Alice's Adventures in Wonderland,* chapters 9 and 10.

Figure 8. Carroll's illustration of the Gryphon and Mock Turtle in *Alice's Adventures under Ground,* chapter 4.

Figure 5 manifests the great (and dangerous) opportunities *Alice's Adventures in Wonderland* offers for sexually oriented, Freudian analysis. More important, these three illustrations (the two on the left from Carroll's own *under Ground* drawings) help reveal how much more frightening is the narrative than readers would guess from viewing only the Tenniel version. The center drawing is especially horrifying because of Alice's bland expression—her dreamy acceptance of the completely bizarre disintegration of orderly identity (compare here Gregor Samsa's phlegmatic "acceptance" of his incredible metamorphosis into a giant insect in Kafka's *The Metamorphosis*). The facial expression in Figure 6 serves the same function: Alice's dreamlike complacency is slightly funny but very frightening as well, and Carroll's illustration is thereby closer to the spirit of the underground adventures than are most of Tenniel's generally pleasant confections.

Figure 2 perhaps best illustrates my thesis. These two pictures illustrate exactly the same incident. Carroll's original filled an entire page, a graphic rendering of Alice's position in the threatening text where there is simply no more space, no margin into which Alice can grow; Tenniel's takes less than half the page, thus scaling down the scene's implications and threats. Carroll's growing Alice—in her fetal position, so horribly crowded in the womblike space she cannot escape—has the same dreamy look of terribly sad acceptance pictured in Figure 6. Tenniel's Alice, on the other hand, tends to dispel the reader's consternation while displaying her own with a cute, rather innocent pout. Moreover, Tenniel's little casement window offers a good deal of comfort to the conscious and unconscious anxieties of any perturbed readers, whether they be children or adults.

Figure 7 contrasts *under Ground*'s Mock Turtle and Gryphon with their *Wonderland* counterparts. In the *Wonderland* pictures they are thoroughly ridiculous; in the *under Ground* picture they seem menacing. Tenniel, celebrated in his day for his political animal cartoons in *Punch*, deftly reveals the patently artificial, and therefore unthreatening, nature of these mythical creatures: the oxtail and bovine head reveal the true mock nature of the imitation turtle soup—and the false sentiment of the turtle himself, large as he is. Figure 8, from *under Ground,* showing Alice so small in comparison to the creatures, contrasts dramatically with the amusing pas de trois of *Wonderland* in Figure 7. Again, Tenniel sugars over the inherent horrors, emphasizing the surface joys.

Of course, this matter of illustrations is not so clear-cut as it might at first seem: some of Tenniel's illustrations are a bit disturbing, and one or two might even be considered more disturbing than Carroll's counterparts. But by and large the issue is clear: Carroll's powerful, relatively spontaneous illustrations express clearly the threatening implications of his comic nightmare.

POLARITIES

Carroll's comedy, especially in *Alice's Adventures in Wonderland,* rests on a number of polarities embedded in its narrative technique, its verbal texture, its dual perspective—polarities of sense vs. nonsense, consciousness vs. the unconscious, satire vs. sentimentality, waking vs. dreaming, reality vs. fantasy, adult vs. child, narrator vs. protagonist, teller vs. doer, delight vs. fear, pain vs. pleasure, attraction vs. repulsion, order vs. chaos, and laughter vs. tears. From the beginning (including Carroll's sentimental prefatory poem that contrasts so abruptly with the matter-of-fact and highly satirical adventures themselves), these polarities create force fields and tensions immediately disturbing but finally resolved with a dynamically comic solution.

In one of those terribly childish puns in chapter 9, "The Mock Turtle's Story," Carroll himself alludes obliquely to the polar nature of his own comedy. There the Gryphon tells Alice that he went to "the Classical master" at school. "He was an old crab, *he* was," the Gryphon says (we are reminded of Charles Dodgson's own short, unsuccessful career as a crabby mathematics instructor at Oxford). The Mock Turtle answers with a sigh, "I never went to [the Classical master]. He taught Laughing and Grief, they used to say" (W, 77). The correspondences between "Latin and Greek" and "Laughing and Grief" are of course wholly nonsensical, perhaps a bit insane. But laughing and grief, as they manifest themselves in our waking and dreaming lives, are as inextricably related as the multiple, incongruous threads of our mock-epic existence woven together into that whole comic fabric we so wonder at in Carroll's *Alices*.

8

"And here I must leave you": Death, Love, and the White Knight's Farewell*

> . . . unless this miracle have might,
> That in black ink my love may still shine bright.
> —Shakespeare, Sonnet 65

Throughout his adult life, Charles Dodgson devoted a great measure of his time, energy, and wealth to his love for little girls.[1] Moreover, as a true amateur par excellence, in his everyday affairs and amusements, and throughout his letters, diaries, and lesser literary works—from the satirical "Love's Railway Guide" (ca. 1844) of his juvenilia to his final maudlin opus *Sylvie and Bruno Concluded* (1893), which ends with an angel's voice whispering "IT IS LOVE"—love was clearly one of his dominant concerns. As he wrote to an 11-year-old correspondent when he was 59, "love is the best thing in all the world" (*Letters*, 869).

Love was also a crucial topic in Dodgson's milieu, a late-Romantic world where a number of despairing Oxford contemporaries, like his fellow Rugby graduate Matthew Arnold, had already retreated to personal love as the only secure refuge on the "darkling plain" of their faithless, increasingly mechanical, and morally anarchic age ("Dover Beach," Arnold's famous, poignant poem on this subject,

---

*This chapter is based on "Love and Death in Carroll's *Alices*," in *English Language Notes* 20, no. 2 (December 1982): 26–45.

was written in the early 1850's and published in 1867, two years after *Wonderland* and four years before *Looking-Glass*).

It would therefore seem appropriate to expect much about love in the *Alice* books, and, superficially at least, they seem to satisfy that expectation. The frame story of *Alice's Adventures in Wonderland* ends (as does the frame story of the *under Ground* manuscript) with remarks about Alice's "simple and loving heart" (*W*, 99); *Through the Looking-Glass* begins with a prefatory poem declaring that Charles Dodgson's "love-gift of a fairy-tale" will elicit a "loving smile" from his dearest erstwhile little reader, Alice Liddell (*L*, 103). Within Alice's adventures themselves, THE KING AND QUEEN OF HEARTS (*W*, 63) stand prominently capitalized at the center of the punning world of Wonderland. Moreover, a child protagonist like Alice seems to de-mand a loving emotional response from adult readers. In addition, love also lies at the base of several of those nursery rhymes Alice unwittingly subverts. And despite the Cheshire Cat's assertion that madness reigns in Wonderland, the Ugly Duchess declares with equal finality, " 'tis love, 'tis love, that makes the world go round!" (*W*, 70).

But Alice, in much the same uncontrollable way that she twists the loving and sentimental messages of her nursery rhymes into dark *Wonderland* visions of unloving, predatory, post-Darwinian nature, reminds the insincere Duchess of the Duchess's own earlier declara-tion: the world goes round, Alice suggests, "by everybody minding their own business!" (*W*, 70). Indeed, Alice's curt, unloving deflation of love here mirrors an important facet of Carroll's characteristically antisentimental approach to love in the *Alices*. Despite the great care Dodgson expended in preparing the beautiful *under Ground* manu-script as a love gift for his dear Alice Liddell, his final drawing, near the end of the manuscript, was of the mad Queen of Hearts (see Figure 3), whom he later called a heartless "blind and aimless Fury,"[2] as alien from love and love gifts as any fantasy creature could conceivably be. And inside the *Alice* adventures, the love that the books might be expected to endorse seems to have no better prospect for survival than do any of the other admirable motives and principles that underlie and make our world go round and that collapse so easily when subjected to cool, cynical, detached Carrollian satire in the topsy-turvy madhouses of Dodgson's invention.

The quest structures of both *Alices* graphically represent a failed search for the warm joy and security of love. Once inside Wonderland, Alice desperately seeks to enter the "loveliest garden you ever saw"— that is, for almost everyone in Carroll's original audience, the Garden of Eden. But instead of getting to that tranquil, secluded place of secure and perfect love, Alice finds herself in the Queen of Hearts' croquet grounds, a place of perfect (albeit laughable) hate and fury— like a comic rendition of William Blake's embittered "Garden of Love," an ironically perverted, dreadfully confused version of the paradise the child in us seeks in its joys and desires. In *Through the Looking-Glass*, which contains several positive but fleeting images of love, Alice's quest for queenhood does not meet with exactly the same frustration, but it too ends in "dreadful confusion," which Alice must escape because she "can't stand [it] any longer!" (*L*, 204). Being a queen behind the looking-glass, Alice discovers, offers little solace to a seeker after love.

Thus, Alice's worlds under the ground and behind the mirror turn out to be, it seems, nonsensical places without love, places of terrifying separation and loneliness. It is no wonder that in both books Alice cries bitter tears engendered by that loneliness: "I am so *very* tired of being all alone here!" (*W*, 17) she sobs in Wonderland; and with a "melancholy voice" behind the looking-glass, she cries, "it is so *very* lonely here!" (*L*, 152).

QUESTIONS RAISED

These apparent contradictions raise some important critical questions: Why, in view of Carroll's declared purposes for his *Alice* books and in view of much more literary, historical, and biographical evidence, do the *Alice* narratives appear to frustrate almost every impulse toward love—even the impulses their own frames excite? Why does love within the *Alices* exist, apparently, only fitfully and only in self-centered, infantile forms or in places where, so to speak, things have no names? More specifically, how can these texts be framed by so much love and yet apparently exclude love from their central stories? Finally, why do readers tend to remember the *Alices*, despite all this evidence to the contrary, as somehow warm, even loving, experiences and Alice herself as the embodiment of Dodgson's own later vision of her: "What wert thou, dream-Alice, in thy foster-father's eyes? How shall he picture thee? Loving, first, loving and gentle: loving as a dog (forgive the prosaic simile, but I know no earthly love so pure and perfect), and gentle as a fawn."[3]

Elizabeth Sewell's celebrated study of Carroll and Edward Lear, *The Field of Nonsense* (1952),[4] explains why love has no place in nonsense, why, indeed, love and nonsense are ultimately incompatible. Sewell's argument rests on the firm premise that nonsense is game; consequently, *Alice in Wonderland* and *Through the Looking-Glass* (for Sewell, eminent examples of English nonsense) must turn all life, all fluid human emotions, everything, into cold, discrete, static counters for play within a closed field. The nonsense world inside the *Alices*, claims Sewell, "is not a universe of things but of words and ways of using them, plus a certain amount of pictorial illustration. In Nonsense all the world is paper and all the seas are ink" (Sewell, 17).

Bearing in mind that the games in the *Alices* often involve kinetic, changing counters, rather than the static ones required for the game of nonsense postulated by Sewell (and accepted by a variety of critics as an apt description of Carroll's comic power);[5] keeping in mind, for example, those wriggling, live-animal mallets and balls of Wonderland croquet or the lively and talkative chess pieces of Looking-Glass chess, we can nevertheless pursue Sewell's argument profitably. For her, the *Alices* constitute "a work about itself" (Sewell, 21–22). Thus, love—whether as a serious subject or as a substantial conceptual element with more than mere game-counter applications or as the spirit (style, tone, manner, etc.) in which the game of nonsense is played—has no place whatsoever in, indeed is subversive of, the game world we must enter when we enter the nonreferential fields of Edward Lear's poetry or Lewis Carroll's "Jabberwocky." What we understand by human love (unlike, incidentally, Dodgson's "pure and perfect" love of dog or fawn) is fiercely kinetic, its kinesis and imperfection dominating the subject matter of Western literature since at least the Renaissance. Furthermore, no instance of human love is ever (as every game counter must be) entirely discrete, ever fully completed, ever isolated, ever merely "about itself." Indeed, the conception of love we inherit from the Romantics depends heavily on the principle of incompleteness and on dreams of unattainable mergers between ordinarily discrete entities and selves (in our day represented most often by sexual unions; in Carroll's day represented most vividly in the operatic vision of love celebrated in romantic fictions, *Wuthering Heights* [1847] being a striking example). A game uses separate entities as playthings. According to Sewell, "The Nonsense universe must be the sum of its parts and nothing more" (Sewell, 98). Love, like imagination, seeks to dissolve separation and to engender syntheses greater than the sums of their parts.

If we accept Sewell's definition, we must understand love to be in a sense destructive of nonsense, the warm emotional force that naturally resists taking the world the way nonsense presumably takes it— as simply a congeries of cold, permanently discrete "units going one and one and one" (Sewell, 67). Love works like a solvent, dissolving isolation and breaking down separateness, making the world more fluid and less static, tending toward fusion and away from discreteness. Therefore, a quest for love in the nonsensical *Alice*s, like Alice's nonsensical quest for the tranquil innocence of the lovely garden or for the permanent freedom of adult queenhood, seems nonsensical too and—appropriately—destined to fail. Hence it would appear that the warm, unsatirized (and sometimes sentimental) love that permeates the frame materials of the *Alice*s and that is sometimes ridiculed within their narratives has no place within the narratives and is finally extraneous and alien to their central purposes.

ROMANCEMENT

A useful gloss on these matters appears in one of Carroll's minor early fictions, "Novelty and Romancement" (published in *The Train* in

1856 when Dodgson was 24 and just getting used to his new pen name).[6] "Novelty and Romancement" is the first-person account of one Leopold Edgar Stubbs (among other things, a caricature of an overly romantic Edgar Allan Poe narrator-hero), a young man with a feverish imagination and an all-consuming "thirst and passion . . . for poetry, for beauty, for novelty, for romancement" (1080). The target of derision, a sentimentalist mercilessly lampooned by Carroll's antiromantic irony, Stubbs serves as a satiric representation of the spirit motivating the Romantic love quest—the love of love itself. The cream of Carroll's rather facile jest depends on Stubbs's dim-witted belief that the "romancement" he so ardently seeks (compare here Alice's two quests or the futile hunting of the Snark) is to be found in a mechanic's shop on Great Wattles-street: he spies the sign "Simon Lubkin. Dealer in Romancement" and thinks he has found the dear object of his lifelong quest. "Romancement" (here read "love"), he fondly believes, can be bought like herring or glue from a common shopman.

The climax of "Novelty and Romancement" comes when Stubbs, "with a throbbing and expectant heart," discovers that he has been "deluded by a heated imagination": he has, in his youthful ardor, misread the shopkeeper's sign. What he had read on the sign as "Romancement" was all along merely "Roman cement." Until the story's denouement, he had never seen the "hideous gap" yawning between the N and the C, "making it not one word but two!" (1087–88). Instead of the fused and fusing "romancement" Stubbs has passionately sought, he finds only "Roman cement," as cold, hard, and mundane a conception as the two discrete terms used to signify it. Stubbs is obviously from beginning to end a romantic fool, but his "phantom hope" for "romancement," the childish dream he held with an "expectant heart," is no more foolish than is the dream image of a forever seven-year-old Alice that haunted Dodgson "phantomwise" (*L*, 209), or the imaginative quests that motivated Alice— or the object of warm love any one of us might cherish in a young and hopeful imagination. Before Stubbs discovers the sad truth, Lubkin innocently tells him what the stuff in his shop is used for: "It would piece a most anything together." Stubbs of course misunderstands Lubkin's straightforward remark, thinking it refers to the spirit of "romancement," a spirit, he imagines, that "serves to connect the broken threads of human destiny" (1084)—a view of human love consistent with much that Dodgson wrote in many of his letters, diary entries, poetry, and fictions.

The emotional-imaginative cement fusing two separate, lifeless, prosaic terms—"roman" and "cement"—in Stubbs's poetic and "fertile imagination" (1084) suddenly loses its cohesive powers and its fertility: the frigid, isolated words fly apart into separate dead counters in the unimaginative games of commerce and commercial discourse. The now-experienced Stubbs puts it neatly at the end, without for once his florid prose: "the dream was over" (1088). Like a reversed mirror image of the sudden endings and the protective, sentimental frame stories that tend to encapsulate and thus defuse Alice's two threatening dream quests, this abrupt conclusion to "Novelty and Romancement" also widens the gap between romance and frightening reality, in this case reducing the warm and fusing love of Stubbs's central story to a mere misreading of separate and lifeless signs. As it so often is in Carroll's fictions, romanticism is here comically represented as a matter of poor eyesight—sentimentality that falsifies our views of reality. The unitary vision of a coherent, dynamic world alive and turning on the power of love is shattered into the hideous but businesslike perception of a "real" world of "broken threads" that goes round because each entity (and each word) remains separate, minding its "own business," pursuing its own survival, while each seeker of love's coherence and order remains a fool like Stubbs, permanently isolated in his solitary and loveless prison.

The old signs, the old words declaring love's fusing magic, like the words on Simon Lubkin's sign proclaiming his prosaic wares, fall before cleared vision into their morally meaningless, discrete parts. "Novelty and Romancement" ends both sadly and satirically, with a final gibe at Poe: "The signboard yet creaks upon the moldering wall, but its sound shall make music in these ears nevermore—ah! nevermore" (1088).

LOSING ALICE

Nevertheless, a quest for the sustained and sustaining music of love inside the frame stories of the *Alices* need not end with a frustrating, nonsensical Boojum, the cacophonous creak of a misread sign. The eighth chapter of *Through the Looking-Glass* ("It's My Own Invention") yields some promising results. And, in spite of the apparent incoherent randomness of Carroll's seemingly disjointed nonsense materials, this chapter even suggests for the *Alices* the possibility of a satisfying completeness and moral shape. Besides finding in "It's My Own Invention" some of the best evidence of the loving nature that Dodgson claimed was his heroine's chief virtue, we witness in this late, concluding episode something that, in terms of a search for love, is much more significant—a response to that loving nature in the only genuine, fully human exchange within all of Alice's adventures: a poignantly brief, touchingly realistic farewell between a foolish old White Knight and Alice, that Knight's beloved seven-and-a-half-year-old maiden in distress. (It should be emphasized that the White Knight, a proper but silly, upper-middle-class protector of young girls, is, as many Carroll scholars agree, one of Dodgson's best self-portraits. Moreover, the emotional matrix of this scene is one with which any reader of Dodgson's letters and diaries will be familiar.)

At this late and pivotal point in her adventures underground and behind the looking-glass, Carroll's imprisoned pawn-princess is freed and is now about to awaken to autonomous queenhood (the next chapter is called simply "Queen Alice"). Meanwhile, Alice's thinly disguised creator Carroll/Dodgson (after surreptitiously admitting that she too is his "own invention") prepares to lose his Galatea forever as she races off eagerly to adulthood and out of the dream worlds he has lovingly invented for her, worlds from which real death was banished and in which her natural aging process had been slyly slowed to a Wonderland rate closer to his heart's desire—a mere half-year's maturation for something like every nine years on the other side of the looking-glass.[7] Carroll's sadly ineffectual persona, meantime, that aged and impotent Prince Charming, that familiar nonsense inventor, the ever-falling, pitiable White Knight, sings his last song and bumbles off toward some isolated and ridiculous death:

> As the Knight sang the last words of the ballad, he gathered up the reins, and turned his horse's head along the road by which they had come. "You've only a few yards to go," he said, "down the hill and over that little brook, and then you'll be a Queen—But you'll stay and see me off first?" he added as Alice turned with an eager look in the direction to which he pointed. "I shan't be long. You'll wait and wave your handkerchief when I get to that turn in the road? I think it'll encourage me, you see." (*L*, 190)

In this chapter, Carroll finally brings to the surface and objectifies for his readers what he has previously only dimly hinted at in Alice's journeys through the loveless realms of heartless queens and unfeeling flat characters from the worlds of nonsense game and nursery rhyme. Until now, the only possible evidence of real love, it seemed, had been so deeply buried in the nonsense adventures that the keynote of the *Alice*s seemed to be *lovelessness*. Until this late episode of Carroll's last *Alice*, the only conceivable manifestation of love was in the narrative act itself—the narrator's gentle structuring of the inherently unstructurable, separate, discrete components of Alice's dreams into a plotted, pleasurably coherent text—a love gift that provides Alice and the reader with a fictive shape that allows them to survive with some measure of sanity in the mad worlds of the adventures and of life itself. Now, however, in the poignant passage just quoted, love is fully represented within the story.

Before continuing, however, let us turn for a moment to Carroll's prefatory poem, specifically to a passage that promises his readers a particular emotional immunity. The poem ends:

> And, though the shadow of a sigh
> May tremble through the story,
> For "happy summer days" gone by,
> And vanish'd summer glory—
> It shall not touch, with breath of bale,
> The pleasance of our fairy-tale.
>
> (*L*, 103)

The narrative following this promise, however, fails to sustain such an emotional immunity. Indeed, the emotional charge underlying the haunting farewell between the White Knight and Alice is so powerful it breaks through the neat nonsense surfaces of "It's My Own Invention," perhaps the most nonsensical episode of Alice's adventures, letting readers hear distinctly a different but vaguely familiar tone—that nostalgic "shadow of a sigh," which, though we hardly suspected it, has, as Carroll admits, "tremble[d] through the story" ever since Alice first followed another Dodgson alter ego, the timid white Rabbit, down the rabbit hole.

The intrusion of such a nostalgic "sigh," faint as it is, subverts Carroll's own intention to give his audience (particularly Alice herself) a love gift of gamelike, pure, nonsensical pleasure untouched by any breath of "bale" or any warm, fluid emotions that can threaten the static discreteness on which the "pleasance" of nonsense games rests. (In Dodgson's day, incidentally, "pleasance" signified, among other things, [1] a pleasant, unthreatening emotional experience, [2] for him, Alice *Pleasance* Liddell, his real-girl love, and [3], a secluded garden.) Admitting to the field of nonsense an emotion as alien as nostalgia risks opening its pleasant seclusion to other disturbing strangers, among them Death. Here in chapter 8 Death is no longer a fictive stranger, a mere uncharged sign and discrete counter for endless games where "they never executes nobody" and where Death's agent Time can itself die, or stop dead forever in a laughable, unending mad tea party. And the "voice of dread" that, as Carroll's poem reminds us, inevitably "summon[s] to unwelcome bed" every "melancholy maiden"[8] also breaks through, becoming manifest for the only time in all the adventures yet thereby revealing that it has been a dynamic element from the beginning—singing quietly, hurrying near, at the back of Carroll's rushing tales about Alice's "nonsensical" experiences of life, love and disorder.

Carroll understood well the threat such a "breath of bale" poses for nonsense games. Consciously, he believed that the approaching, inexorable "bedtime" to which his poem alludes must not, would not, play any part in the adventures. But in "It's My Own Invention" the baleful "frost," the "raving blast" of fall and winter, which is often the catalyst for human love, comes alive dramatically in the comic narrative's overt, realistic portrayals of aging, old age, and falling to earth (the text alludes to the old Knight's falling at least 30 times), as well as in its covert plays on the word "grave" and its many references to gravity—a no-nonsense, inescapable force pulling us all down to earth and our common resting place. And the pervasive, melancholy tone that conveys all this—the emotional aura suffusing this autumnal scene, reaching its climax with the spectacle of an aged man (not a mere nonsense creature, but a *man*) singing as his final love gift for a departing child his nonsense song "The Aged Aged Man"— reveals finally, and with a sharp immediacy, the suppressed pathos that has subtly informed both *Alice* books, making them something much more referential, much richer and more human than the insulated, indeterminate nonsense that constitutes their surface. Paradoxically, this grave tone emanates from Carroll's fortunate failure to keep his nonsense pure and free from that "shadow of a sigh" he himself admits in his poem. The tone emanates from a deep, abiding sense that human love springs from time and human mortality. Hardly a fit subject for the closed playing fields of nonsense, but just the right subject for books quoted as often as Shakespeare's sonnets on love, death, and the power of the word.

LOVE AND DEATH

Much of the love Dodgson bore for the innumerable little Alices of his own fleeting life was of a kind adult readers know well. His letters and diaries (and several of his lesser literary works) are fully open about that sense of advancing age that makes us "love that well which [we] must leave ere long." The depth and intensity of Dodgson's preoccupation with this particular pain can be gauged by how heavily it is emphasized in this structurally crucial chapter, especially in the chapter's continual iteration of two intertwined motifs—old age and falling. Like Shakespeare's May-time beloved beholding the final decline of a wintertime lover, like middle-aged Humbert Humbert's pitiful adoration of his indifferent nymphet Lolita fading before him into a future he cannot share, like the many literary celebrations of the love that springs from fallen humanity's futile, doomed race against world and time, against the imprisoning Biological Trap or the "blight man was born for," the *Alice* books, despite their sprightly surface nonsense, have all along whispered of love's intimate relations with inevitable death, but so faintly and subtly that the effect is necessarily—and appropriately—subliminal. In this sunset chapter of the final *Alice,* however, in this autumnal and peculiarly isolated scene of final parting between a (foster) father and the child he has in great measure created, the grave underlying themes of old age, evanescent and unrequited love, and youth's impatience for autonomous life break through for a brief moment to become the vivid mainstream and audible melody of Carroll's narrative.

We now know that Carroll intended to intensify these themes and make them even more explicit in this chapter: with a characteristic *Looking-Glass* doubling, he planned (although he was finally dissuaded by Tenniel) to add immediately after the White Knight episode a parallel scene of young Alice parting from another aged, aged man— the even older, dying Wasp in a Wig, who sings a pitiable and sometimes gruesome song about his own last days:

> So now that I am old and gray,
> And all my hair is nearly gone,
> They take my wig from me and say
> "How can you put such rubbish on?"[9]

But although the Wasp episode does bear a number of similarities to the White Knight section, it might not appear to be about love. For while the "very unhappy," working-class Wasp represents the sadness of approaching death (being November behind the looking-glass, it is already well past the "unwelcome bedtime" of most wasps) and while Alice again represents lively youth impatient for impending maturity (she turns back to the aged Wasp "rather unwillingly, for she was very anxious to be a Queen"), readers might nevertheless find it difficult to discover in this Wasp fragment any hint of the love-out-of-death theme I have described in this chapter. Read in context, however, the distinct change Alice's polite indulgence effects in this irascible old creature represents a sudden engendering of warm human emotion in the coldest, most rigid, most elderly figure in Carroll's extensive collection of cranky, inflexible, waspish grown-ups. In the final words of this episode, the Wasp suddenly reaches emotionally toward Alice, displaying genuine civility—a subtle sign that for the shy, socially fastidious Dodgson could convey private love: "Good-bye, and thank-ye," said the Wasp, and Alice tripped down the hill again, quite pleased that she had gone back and given a few minutes to making the poor old creature comfortable" (*Wasp*, 21). Such civility—here in response to Alice's acts of authentic noblesse oblige for a "poor creature" of the lower orders (lower biologically, socially, morally)—coming from such an improbable source, represents the widely held Victorian belief in the miraculous regenerative power loving childhood could offer to the dying old. This spiritual solvent could teach grown-ups to love—even at the last moments—offering the means to liberate them from their class-conscious emotional rigidity and isolation, as it so often liberated Charles Dodgson from his.[10]

In any case, Carroll's concentration on his peculiar version of the eros-thanatos principle, his bittersweet and sentimental vision of a fallen old man's innocent and fruitless love for an even more innocent, unattainable child, shapes many features of "It's My Own Invention." And comprehending Carroll's strategies for transforming that vision into the nonsensical parting of a ludicrous White Knight from an eager Alice—a parting that also announces the approaching end of his *Alices* and, perhaps, of their loving inventor—helps illuminate the shy but ardent love that trembles softly through the *Alices*.

In "It's My Own Invention" Carroll dramatizes a strikingly realistic encounter between two human figures as familiar in literary convention as they are in ordinary life: the aged, inept, foolish, and sometimes doting male lover, and the indifferent, impatient, lively young female object of his love. Screened by fantasy, Carroll's treatment of this traditional material differs widely from the sentimental versions with which his original adult audience was most familiar. But many of the convention's principal elements operate in Carroll's fantastic rendition. For example, what is often emphasized in such a couple (for pathetic and tragic as well as for comic purposes) is their essential incompatibility. Here that incompatibility is deftly exaggerated and curiously elaborated. Alice, for instance, looks upon the aged Knight as a laughable old fool, but she takes great pains to conceal her youthful amusement and "dares not laugh" at him; she generously allows him to mistake her "puzzled" thoughts about his ridiculous invention of a platonic pudding for "sad" thoughts about her eagerly awaited departure (L, 186). The Knight, for his part, considers his sentimental and funny song beautifully sad, while, upon hearing it, Alice finds "no tears [come] into her eyes" (L, 187); and even he is forced to observe gently, "but you didn't cry so much as I thought you would" (L, 190). From all of this emerges a subtle, curious emotional exchange, a loving mutuality that has not been openly manifested before in the adventures and one that, on Alice's side, represents far more than just her well-bred politeness. The fleeting love whispering through this scene is therefore complicated and paradoxical: it is a doomed love between a girl-child all potential, freedom, flux, and growing up and a pitiable, elderly man-child all impotence, imprisonment, stasis, and falling down.

While the doddering but cavalier White Knight's continual falling and his outlandish horsemanship also suggest sexual impotence (his name is a pun on a familiar term for a sleepless night—a "white night"—in the context of these fecund dream visions itself a mark of stasis and impotence), that falling bears a more immediate and wider reference to other sharp contrasts between him and Alice, who has now attained the ability to manage, with the evanescent grace of childhood, some rather tricky matters of gravity and balance. Indeed, much of the conversation here sounds as if Alice is now the knowing grown-up and the Knight the innocent child (a role reversal repeated throughout her *Looking-Glass* adventures with many childish grown-ups). Considering his propensity for falling, for example, Alice at one point declares, "You ought to have a wooden horse on wheels, that you ought!" and he sheepishly asks, "Does that kind go smoothly?" (*L*, 184). It is this sort of second-childhood childishness, the White Knight's near-senile frailty and dependence on a fickle child, that makes him laughable here and at the same time pitiable (surely an undesirable fusion in the game of nonsense). But more than anything else, the utter hopelessness of his attachment to the departing child makes him a haunting figure of universal reference.

Dodgson was not yet 40 when he was writing and publishing what he undoubtedly recognized as his final *Alice* book, but already he thought of himself as a rather aged man whose "wells of . . . imagination [would] soon run dry" (*Letters*, 181). This premature sense of old age and sterility appears early and often in his diaries and letters, and it comes to the surface with considerable tragicomic force in "It's My Own Invention." For one thing, aging implies the loss of imaginative strength, what might be called the generative power of creative "invention." Carroll considered his great works of fantasy, like his dreams, free gifts of a youthful and unfettered imagination. At the age of 55 and looking back on his career, he described the process of developing in his early 30s his oral *under Ground* stories into the book we know as *Alice in Wonderland:*

> To please a child I loved (I don't remember any other motive), I printed in manuscript, and illustrated with my own crude designs . . . the book [*Alice's Adventures under Ground*] which I have just had published in facsimile [1886]. In writing it out, I added many fresh ideas, which seemed to grow of themselves upon the original stock; and many more added themselves when, years afterwards, I wrote it all over again for publication: but (this may interest some readers of "Alice" to know) every such idea and nearly every word of the dialogue, *came of itself.* Sometimes an idea comes at night, when I have had to get up and strike a light to note it down—sometimes when out on a lonely winter walk, when I have had to stop, and with half-frozen fingers jot down a few words which should keep the new-born idea from perishing—but whenever or however it comes, *it comes of itself.* I cannot set invention going like a clock, by any voluntary winding up. . . . "Alice" and

the "Looking-Glass" are made up almost wholly of bits and scraps, single ideas which came of themselves. Poor they may have been; but at least they were the best I had to offer.[11]

In this context, "It's My Own Invention" can be read as the White Knight Inventor Dodgson's self-mocking but sad farewell to the creative powers inspired by his beloved muse Alice—Alice, the living symbolic force of love in his younger life who provided the emotional energy, the psychic cement to hold the "bits and scraps" of his restless and unfocused inventive fancy together in a meaningful shape, a plotted story, an edifice of Romancement rather than of Roman cement. Now that the child Alice has grown away from him into womanhood, the poor old White Knight is to be left with his *own* paltry, merely mechanical inventions, which, without the living Alice, become unworkable gadgets and silly, sterile toys. Wakeful and dreamless like a "white night," alone and bereft of his lovable inspiration, he feels incapable of recapturing the fluid dreaming spirit that once, when his "summer suns were glowing," empowered him to invent freely tales that "came of themselves," retaining the "vanish'd summer glory" (*L*, 103) inspired by a child he dearly loved.

"Glory" might be merely a "nice knock-down argument" for Humpty Dumpty (*L*, 163), but for Dodgson here—and for William Wordsworth whom he continually honors and mocks in "It's My Own Invention" and elsewhere in the *Alices*[12]—"glory" is a pregnant term, connoting that quality of creative imagination that offers, particularly in childhood, a precious sense of interpenetration with nature and with those one loves. Wordsworth believed that such an original summertime "glory" can be recaptured so that adults, although far "inland" in their progress to their graves, can sometimes see, imaginatively, "the Children sport upon the shore, / And hear the mighty waters rolling evermore."[13] For the aging Dodgson, who so loved children and childhood, that glory seems irretrievably lost in the desiccating aging process, the free-flowing inventiveness that springs from it permanently dried up.

Alice has already learned that "one can't help growing older" (*L*,

162), even if the childish Knight has in his dotage apparently forgotten that dreadful fact. The middle-aged Dodgson of course knows it too well. For all his jokes about living backwards behind the looking-glass, his final *Alice* book and especially "It's My Own Invention" make it perfectly clear that age and impotence will have their way, that the seminal "wells of fancy" will be inevitably "drained . . . dry" (*W*, 3), as are the seminal dreams that, as he emphasizes, come "of themselves" and are never merely mechanical products of the artist's *own*, unaided, cerebral "invention."

Several of the White Knight's ludicrous inventions—like his hilarious plan for keeping his hair from falling off (compare the more aged Wasp in a Wig whose hair is now almost completely gone)—represent futile attempts to defy both gravity and time. From the first episode in *under Ground* to this final episode of *Through the Looking-Glass*, Carroll, too, has with his own inventions attempted covertly to defy the inescapable forces pulling us to the grave. But in "It's My Own Invention" he seems to flirt with a nearly overt admission of defeat, inspiring Alice's laughter at his White Knight's foolish attempts to avoid nature's implacable regimen. Dodgson's chief inventions— Lewis Carroll's *Alices*—were, this chapter seems to say, no more successful at preserving Dodgson's love or preventing Alice Liddell from growing beyond him and toward death than are the White Knight's schemes to avoid falling or the Aged Aged Man's "design / To keep the Menai bridge from rust / By boiling it in wine" (*L*, 189).

When the courtly Knight, "a faint smile lighting up his gentle foolish face" (*L*, 187), sings his parting song for Alice, readers might easily overlook, in all its nonsense, these deadly serious, commonsensical aspects of the song and of the entire sunset scene. But Alice is not so insensitive. She somehow grasps the episode's strange gravity:

Of all the strange things that Alice saw in her journey Through the Looking-Glass, this was the one that she always remembered most clearly. Years afterwards she could bring the whole scene back again, as if it had been only yesterday—the mild blue eyes and kindly smile of the Knight—the setting sun gleaming through his hair . . . and the black shadows of the forest behind—all this she took in like a picture . . . listening, in a half-dream, to the melancholy music of the song (L, 187).

Half dreaming, the open-hearted Alice has heard the poignant, hopeless love of "The Aged Aged Man" pulsing secretly beneath the song's surface nonsense. Moreover, as Carroll subtly suggests, there is a reasonable chance that the real Alice Liddell (in her own "half-dream," halfway between her actual listening, reading, waking self and her fantasy self inside the dream fiction) has heard similarly that same "melancholy music of the song," that same unfulfillable love, throughout the comical adventures—Dodgson's trembling, grave "shadow of a sigh" that makes Carroll's best "nonsense" timeless and universal in ways far beyond the reach of unreferential nonsense.

The tune of "The Aged Aged Man," as Alice says to herself, "*isn't his own invention*" (L, 187), despite the Knight's claim that it is. The tune (and Alice apparently identifies its source correctly) comes from Thomas Moore's "My Heart and Lute," a poignant Irish love song that surely no seven-and-a-half-year-old could completely understand. As Martin Gardner suggests, "It is quite possible that Carroll regarded Moore's love lyric as the song that he, the White Knight [and Charles Lutwidge Dodgson], would have liked to sing to Alice [and to Alice Pleasance Liddell] but dared not."[14] In any case, Alice's politely unspoken recognition of the underlying Moore love lyric here bespeaks at once her acute child's ear, her high-bred diplomacy, and her precocious sensitivity to the oblique voice of love beneath the song's absurd lyrics and, it is likely, beneath all her absurd fantastic adventures invented by the adoring, "aged," ludicrous White Knight Dodgson.

Moore's song begins, "I give thee all—I can no more— / Though poor the off'ring be. / My heart and lute are all the store / That I can bring to thee." The White Knight's parallel song, beginning "I'll tell thee everything I can," is also a poor offering, like the many poor nonsensical offerings of another aged and silly inventor, also given in tones of modest love to unattainable children impatient for adult life and finally incapable of understanding the pathetic depth of such grown-up melancholy music (compare Dodgson's 1887 remark previously quoted here: "Poor [the *Alices*] may have been; but at least they were the best I had to offer"). Moore's singer sings of a "soul of love" and a "heart that feels / Much more than lute could tell." Carroll's counterpointed nonsense song likewise cannot—must not—tell fully what Dodgson's heart feels. Alice, of course, while capable of recognizing the poignant love song beneath the invented nonsense words, is blessedly incapable of understanding fully what that curious blend of ludicrous words and heartfelt music tells about herself, about the silly old man singing before her, and about the human condition: "She stood and listened very attentively, but no tears came into her eyes" (*L*, 187). Only adults can hear, and only if they listen very attentively, all of Carroll's gravity and melancholy love. Only adults can hear the full sad irony, for example, of this funny exchange between innocent Alice and her experienced White Knight:

> "People don't fall off quite so often, when they've had much practice." "I've had plenty of practice," the Knight said very gravely: "plenty of practice!" (*L*, 183).

END OF THE OLD RULES

The White Knight has had plenty of practice with another kind of falling as well. For history, like the passing of an individual's life, has a way of changing the rules of the game, of making many an old man's most precious values increasingly obsolete to the point of extinction. A painful sense of this kind of cultural and ethical loss, of this sort of fatal falling out of fashion contributes another melancholy motif to the nostalgic undertone of the *Alices*; and again that undertone becomes most audible in the White Knight's poignant farewell.

Dodgson's contemporaries who shared his upper-middle-class ethos were faced by a rapidly accelerating erosion of their conservative, rather static life-styles and class privilege. Desperately seeking permanence and some quiet rest in a period of widespread innovation and brawling social upheaval, they had witnessed in their own lifetimes enormously disturbing, inexorable cultural changes, many of them having profound effects on their more and more outdated views of human relations, of "gentlemanly" manners and knightly noblesse oblige. Matthew Arnold's *Culture and Anarchy* is the best known of a flood of mid-Victorian tracts about the disturbing, massive shifts in human values and human relationships accompanying the revolutionary intellectual, technological, economic, and political changes that characterized the Victorian age. Arnold's call for a return to what he considered a more organic, less mechanical ethos, a "Hellenism" that puts a premium on cultural refinement rather than on getting and spending and material success, often seems from our vantage point rather wistful, outdated, impracticable—a sober (sometimes snobbish) version of the aged White Knight's funny, unworkable inventions and Dodgson's unrealistic schemes for social improvement (such as his published pieces on vivisection and Parliamentary elections). Carroll's comic treatment of these matters in the *Alices*—amid the tension between Alice's "culture" and the creatures' "anarchy"—is conveyed most vividly in the dramatization of a very specific personal relationship between one representative from each of the two upper-middle-class Victorian generations—the aged, anachronistic White Knight and the youthful Alice eager to move ahead in the new, exciting "game . . . being played all over the world" (*L*, 126). But Carroll's treatment also has national, even global implications like those found in the jeremiads of such contemporary Victorian prophets as Carlyle, Arnold, and Ruskin.

In common parlance, the term "White Knight" has for many centuries connoted a chivalrous (often celibate) protector of weak "maidens in distress." In modern parlance, the term has taken on the comic connotations of anachronistic chivalry, of a devotion to social values and gallant altruism that has, with the passage of time and the advent of industrialized capitalism, become unworkable, futile—even silly. Like the White Knight's invention of a pudding that Alice cannot believe "ever was cooked . . . ever *will* be cooked!" (*L*, 186), his chivalry seems, in the hurly-burly of a railroad and telegraph world where time itself is "worth a thousand pounds a minute" (*L*, 129–31), an outlandish, immaterial "invention"—worthy of laughter, perhaps of pity, but not of continued allegiance or admiration.

The White Knight has come to rescue Alice from the Red Knight, whose prisoner she is as the episode opens. " 'Well, we must fight for her, then,' said the Red Knight. . . . 'You will observe the Rules of Battle, of course?' the White Knight remarked, putting on his helmet" (*L,* 179). But the White Knight and his assumption of the chivalric Rules of Battle are funny as old-fashioned, outdated manners are often funny, and pitiable as adherents of anachronistic, idealistic values are often pitiable in an ever-modernizing materialist culture held together now, not by things like knighthood's noblest rules, but by what Carlyle had already in the 1830s called scornfully "the cash nexus." Moreover, youthful Alice is herself in such a terrible rush to move on that, without her knowing it, her own, rather old-fashioned bourgeois rules and manners are also in jeopardy.

Modern inventions had in the earlier Victorian period so sped up and mechanized human lives that Alice's frenetic adventures in the Looking-Glass railway carriage, for instance, were by the 1860s and 1870s, despite their fantastic elements, essentially commonplace occurrences for Carroll's original readers (for example, the British steam railways covered well over 8,000 miles by the time Dodgson told his *under Ground* stories, and telegraph cables linked London instantly with New York and Bombay before the publication of *Through the Looking-Glass*). The material changes in modern living occasioned by new technologies and new wealth were accompanied by vast changes in social class and thus in human relationships, rendering the customs of White Knight chivalry (like the White Knight's inept horsemanship or the courtly Charles Dodgson's old-fashioned, fastidious, conservative manners in his platonic love relations with little girls) silly, or sad—or a little of both.

In *Wonderland,* Dodgson's indisputable persona is the Dodo.[15] The Dodo is even more outdated than a chivalrous White Knight who cannot stay mounted on a horse. Indeed, the Dodo is already extinct: by virtue of Carroll's fantasy, the *Wonderland* Dodo is the sole survivor of a real but now extinct species, extinct because the dodos of the Indian Ocean island of Mauritius failed to adapt to the environmental changes wrought in the late seventeenth century by rapacious European commercial interests. Thus, in the Dodo and White Knight, Dodgson satirizes himself as the last of an "endangered" species incapable of adapting its old-fashioned, class-bound, courtly behavior to the demands and mobility of modern laissez-faire capitalism and ruthless imperialism.

"And here I must leave you . . . You are sad," says the White Knight to Alice; but "in an anxious tone" he adds, "let me sing you a song to comfort you" (L, 186). No one else in Alice's many adventures has ever addressed her this way. It is as if the narrator and the narrator's gentle loving voice have crossed over some fragile boundary between reality and fiction, between Alice's adventures and Carroll's telling of them. It is the White Knight Carroll's last farewell and last love gift to Alice. After this he must, like his inventor Dodgson (who has had plenty of sad practice saying good-bye to real girls entering "queenhood"), continue his well-practiced falling, alone and unaided to the end. In his later years Dodgson writes to a woman who was his friend as a girl and is now about to enter the dubious queenhood of Victorian marriage: "My child-friends are all marrying off, now, terribly quick! But, for a solitary broken-hearted old bachelor, it is certainly soothing to find that some of them, even when engaged, continue to write as 'yours affectionately'! But for that, you will easily perceive that my solitude would be simply *desperate*!" (*Letters*, 862).

"Desperate" is perhaps too strong a word here—certainly too strong for a conscientious Victorian clergyman like Dodgson, and probably too strong to describe the White Knight's own parting words and song. But "desperate" is not so wide of the mark: both Alice and the Knight, after all, recognize that "The Aged Aged Man" is full of very "melancholy music." And in many senses so is the nonsensical chapter that contains it. For the impending loneliness, the approaching loss of love and life for which both Dodgson and his "anxious" White Knight have been practicing so long in their inventive imaginations, is far from a laughing matter. It is serious enough to make them both seek soothing comfort and faint hope in the merest crumbs of affection from a loving child's fickle heart.

Carroll's doomed attempts to keep his beloved child friends forever "dreaming as the summers die" (*L*, 209), his brilliant deployment of "magic words" to "hold [them] fast" (*L*, 103), his perfectly composed photographs that try to fix them forever in their rapidly passing youth—all these represent a glorious and futile struggle of loving art against separating time, that most abused and ridiculed figure in Carroll's comic fantasies. In "It's My Own Invention," the full, destructive power of time is finally displayed openly, a power usually well masked by Carroll's sprightly, defensive nonsense. Here the many allusions to time in the *Alices* come into sharp emotional and moral focus, offering suddenly a brief but clear and touching vision of time's human significance—the despised irresistible agent of ludicrous mortality, carnal desire, and admirable love. Nearing 50, Dodgson writes in a letter to an adult friend, "the experience of many years [has] taught me that there are few things in the world so evanescent as a child's love" (*Letters*, 441). The poignantly familiar love of an aged man for a young and innocent child intensifies that evanescence several fold, serving as a powerful symbol for the evanescence and preciousness of all love and of life itself. The terribly brief encounter between a maiden child about to experience for her first time "queenhood" and its concomitant knowledge of sexuality and death's "unwelcome bed" and a loving, protecting but foolish adult who has had "plenty of practice"—that evanescent moment permanently stopped by art's saving magic—should be understood as Carroll's special message to us, his fellow grown-ups: his own covert interpretation of *Through the Looking-Glass,* an interpretation at least as graphic as the Tenniel frontispiece he chose, presumably, to depict the book's central theme of youth and age.

The *Alices* stop time in their surface nonsense, giving the child in their readers and listeners an unthreatened and unthreatening vista of seemingly endless play (like the caucus race or Tweedle brothers' battle), curiously static and full of discrete counters within a safe, closed field. To their adult audience, however, they give something more: they also whisper some sad truths about the world of flux beyond that pleasant field (Carroll's "tremble" seems a better choice than "whisper"). The walls of Carroll's nonsense pleasances are thus constantly, if surreptitiously, breached by time and death and consequently by the love that springs from them both. So while Carroll's love gift of the

Alices helps the child Alice "keep, through all her riper years, the simple and loving heart of her childhood" (*W*, 99), another voice sings softly at the same time to other ears, to those for whom childhood's dreams might already be like a "pilgrim's wither'd wreath of flowers / Pluck'd in a far-off land" (*W*, 4).

Because it breaks open the closed and static field of nonsense with kinetic love, it can be said that Carroll's finest comedy is much better than the cool nonsense he is often credited with. Better because it is about much more than mere nonsense is about; better because it takes account of a familiar human world charged with love and fear of death. And better because it is, finally, morally superior to the most elegantly cerebral nonsense, telling us in tones of love truths about our nature in a manner that somehow makes delight of our foibles and lovely, evanescent joys of our sorrows. Like so much Victorian comedy from Thomas Carlyle and Charles Dickens to George Eliot and George Meredith, Carroll's *Alices* are great and good because they rest finally upon the warm, fusing morality and sentiment the Victorian age cherished as "humor," not upon those surface games that have brought Carroll so much critical esteem in recent years, but which his own age probably would have considered mere entertaining "wit."

Carroll is, therefore, for yet another reason one of the modern world's best writers of subversive comedy—because of his treatment of love. Like his satire, his witty nonsense often subverts love and sentimentality. But in addition, his love subverts his nonsense and satire. In this Carrollian world of mixed-up signs and sensibilities, the question, as one of Carroll's most unloving characters would say, is "which is to be master—that's all" (*L*, 163). Dodgson probably would have chosen love and romance as the masters of nonsense. The more important question of whether or not Carroll would have made the same choice can be answered in only one place, the *Alices* themselves. And these wonderful adventures seem to tell us, finally, that there is no need for any masters here; indeed, neither nonsense, nor death, nor love can master the rich, fused music of all three that makes the peculiar, abiding romancement of the *Alices* so delightfully complex and perennially rewarding.

THE LAST WORD

Carroll probably had the last word, so to speak, on these matters of nonsense, referentiality, time, death, and love in his *Alices*—not exactly in a word, but in a picture. The last words of *Alice's Adventures under Ground* (and of *Alice's Adventures in Wonderland*, too) are these: "remembering her own child-life, and the happy summer days" (*W, 99*). But between those last two discrete but resonating terms "summer" and "days," at the very end of the *under Ground* manuscript sits Carroll's referent herself, the real dream child Dodgson really loved, the real Alice Liddell gazing from her own and Dodgson's "summer days"—out of the 1860s and Dodgson's lovely photograph and right into our eyes.

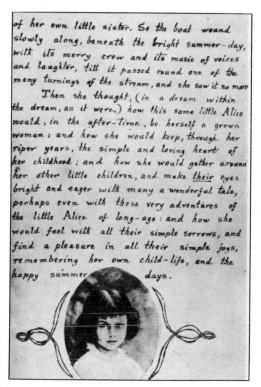

Although this little picture was meant for Alice's eyes alone, it can play an important part in our understanding of love and death in Carroll's *Alices*. For in this haunting photograph of Alice—set into the beautifully handwrought, illustrated *Alice* text and joining (as well as separating) those two, final, discrete words—Carroll embodies the motives and issues that first stirred his heart to create the nonsensical *Alices* and to animate them with a special, curious melancholy music beyond the reach of nonsense. Here before our eyes is his sensitive portrait of the child who is both his heroine and his beloved audience; both a creature in his fictional texts and a real child living outside them; both a thing fashioned from words and the living vessel for the "loving heart of . . . childhood" (*W*, 99). Through the loving devotion of a brilliant and meticulous photographer, Alice here somehow defies time, as if some mad inventor from Alice's dream worlds had, with the magic of his words and art, found a way in her waking world to defy gravity and stop aging and death by means of an improbable Wonderland light-machine and some Looking-Glass Roman-cement.

The *under Ground* photograph records one discrete moment in the actual life of one discrete child. It records that moment without recourse to an inevitably generalizing verbal medium (even the precious name "Alice" is a name many can share). In the wood where things have no names, Alice seems to find for a moment the elusive love she seeks. Here in this picture of his most beloved Alice, Carroll pierces through his own verbal medium to a place beyond names and beyond art, bringing into his text life itself and, in a real sense, the love we all seek—embodied in one specific, real little girl. Whatever else Alice's *under Ground* photograph tells us, it certainly speaks the last word about nonsense, referentiality, time, death, and love in Carroll's *Alices*.

Notes and References

1. The *Alice* Books and Lewis Carroll's World

1. Matthew Arnold, *Culture and Anarchy,* ed. J. Dover Wilson (Cambridge: Cambridge University Press, 1966), 49–50.

2. Alfred, Lord Tennyson, *In Memoriam* (1850), section 56, line 15, in *Tennyson: A Selected Edition,* ed. Christopher Ricks (Berkeley: University of California Press, 1989), 399.

3. Richard D. Altick, *Victorian People and Ideas: A Companion for the Modern Reader of Victorian Literature* (New York: Norton, 1973), 92.

4. Walter Pater, *The Renaissance* (London: Macmillan & Co., 1910; rpt. 1967), 235.

5. Matthew Arnold, "Stanzas from the Grande Chartreuse," in *Poetry and Criticism of Matthew Arnold,* ed. A. Dwight Culler (Boston: Houghton Mifflin, 1961), 187.

6. Matthew Arnold, "Dover Beach," in *Poetry and Criticism of Matthew Arnold,* 161–62.

2. The Importance of the *Alice* Books

1. For example, from 1959 to 1977 at least 24 new Japanese translations of *Alice's Adventures in Wonderland* were published, as well as 23 Italian and 21 Spanish. For a survey of *Alice* translations through the early 1960s, see Warren Weaver, *Alice in Many Tongues: The Translations of "Alice in Wonderland"* (Madison: University of Wisconsin Press, 1964). In "That Girl Is Everywhere" (*New York Times Book Review,* 11 November 1990, 55), Vicki Weissman claims that "*Alice* is the world's most translated book by a single author."

2. *The Lewis Carroll Handbook,* ed. Sidney Herbert Williams, Falconer Madan, and Roger Lancelyn Green (1931); rev. ed., ed. Denis Crutch (Folkstone, Kent, and Hamden, Conn.: Dawson/Archon Books, 1979), 168.

3. *The Letters of Lewis Carroll,* ed. Morton N. Cohen (New York: Oxford University Press, 1979), 548; hereafter cited in the text as *Letters.*

4. (New York and London: Methuen, 1984), xii.

3. Critical Reception of the *Alice* Books

1. Stuart Dodgson Collingwood, *The Life and Letters of Lewis Carroll* (*Rev. C. L. Dodgson*) (New York: Century Co., 1899), 106–7.

2. The *Alice* books should not be credited for initiating the revolt against didactic children's literature, but for bringing to its final flowering a movement begun considerably earlier by such continental children's writers as Charles Perrault, the Grimm brothers, and Hans Christian Andersen; and by English authors like Charles and Mary Lamb, Catherine Sinclair, Charles Dickens, Edward Lear, and John Ruskin. The *Alices* are, in fact, part of a much larger European cultural shift begun long before Carroll's birth, a progressive movement toward a "new, unpietistic handling of childhood" and a rejection of "a whole world of homiletic convention" (G. M. Young, *Victorian England: Portrait of an Age* [1937; rpt. New York: Doubleday, 1954], 229).

3. *Lewis Carroll* (London: Faber & Faber, 1932), 65. Originally published in *The Eighteen Eighties,* ed. Walter De La Mare (Cambridge: Cambridge University Press, 1930).

4. Edmund Wilson, "C. L. Dodson: The Poet Logician," in *The Shores of Light* (New York: Farrar, Straus & Giroux, 1952), 540, 545. Originally published in the *New Republic* (18 May, 1932). Compare William Empson's opening remarks in his famous 1935 essay, "Alice in Wonderland: The Child as Swain": "It must seem a curious thing that there has been so little serious criticism of the Alices, and that so many critics, with so militant and eager an air of good taste, have explained that they would not think of attempting it. Even Mr. De La Mare's book, which made many good points, is queerly evasive in tone. There seems to be a feeling that real criticism would involve psycho-analysis, and that the results would be so improper as to destroy the atmosphere of the books altogether" (*Some Versions of the Pastoral* [London: Chatto & Windus, 1935], 253).

5. Empson, "Alice in Wonderland: The Child as Swain," in *Some Versions of the Pastoral,* 270–71.

6. Rachel Fordyce, *Lewis Carroll: A Reference Guide* (Boston: G. K. Hall, 1988), xxxii.

7. An excellent source for readers wanting to know more about trends in the critical reception of Lewis Carroll is Edward Guiliano's "Lewis Carroll: A Sesquicentennial Guide to Research" (1982). Also useful are Rachel Fordyce's 1988 introduction and Kathleen Blake's "Three Alices, Three Carrolls" in Guiliano and Kincaid's *Soaring with the Dodo* (1982).

4. An Underground Journey to the End of the Night

1. Alice's rapid repetitions of parallel "way" phrases in this sentence—"into the way," "out-of-the-way," and "in the common way"—should be read as a playful, poetic condensation of Alice's rapid, regressive adaptation to the outlandish "ways" of Wonderland: she has voluntarily leaped from the "common way" ("in the world") she and her above-ground fellows commonly pursue, down to the "out-of-the-way" ("out-of-the-world") ways of the new underground, thus getting herself deep "into the way" of Wonderland, a "way" she assumes actually exists. Such subtle word play frequently enriches Carroll's deceptively transparent narrative; it should be watched carefully.

2. See, for example, Alexander L. Taylor, *The White Knight: A Study of C. L. Dodgson (Lewis Carroll)* (London: Oliver & Boyd, 1952), 46–47. Taylor demonstrates how Alice's mathematics are correct because by what she calls her "rate" (i.e., her scale of notation or base, which here is 18), she never would reach 20. He ends his demonstration by asserting, "If the scale of notation was increasing by three at each step and the product by only one, [at] that rate she could never get to 20 at all." A simpler explanation appears in a note on page 38 of Martin Gardner's *The Annotated Alice: Alice's Adventures in Wonderland and Through the Looking-Glass* (New York: Clarkson N. Potter, 1960): "the multiplication table traditionally stops with the twelves, so if you continue this nonsense progression—4 times 5 is 12, 4 times 6 is 13, 4 times 7 is 14, and so on—you end with 4 times 12 (the highest she can go) is 19—just one short of 20."

3. Isaac Watts's original, "Against Idleness and Mischief," was published in 1715 in *Divine Songs for Children* and remained popular throughout the Victorian period:

> How doth the little busy bee
> Improve each shining hour,
> And gather honey all the day
> From every opening flower!
> How skillfully she builds her cell!
> How neat she spreads the wax!
> And labours hard to store it well
> With the sweet food she makes.
>
> In works of labour or of skill,
> I would be busy too;
> For Satan finds some mischief still
> For idle hands to do.
> In books, or work, or healthful play,
> Let my first years be past,
> That I may give for every day
> Some good account at last.

4. Alice's twisted nursery verses usually make far more Darwinian sense than do their original models. See William Empson, "Alice in Wonderland: The Child as Swain," in *Some Versions of the Pastoral*, 253–94, for some provocative comments on the Darwinian theory behind much of Carroll's subversive satire.

5. Compare, for example, the surrealistic trials in Franz Kafka's *The Trial* (1925), Joseph Heller's *Catch-22* (1955), and and E. L. Doctorow's *The Book of Daniel* (1971)—all of these books, incidentally, reveal in many other ways a substantial indebtedness to Carroll's *Alices*.

6. Although watches and clocks that told the day of the month were invented long before the Victorian period, they were still very uncommon in Alice's day. Thus, this remark about the day of the month is meant to be a Wonderland joke.

7. One of English literature's most surrealistic treatments of frozen time, and one that bears close comparison with Carroll's "The Mad Tea-Party," occurs in Dickens's *Great Expectations* (chapter 8) where the naive child protagonist Pip witnesses—in a dark, rather dreamlike, underground vision—Miss Havisham's macabre "party" scene that, like Alice's Wonderland tea party, will never end. "I began to understand," says Pip," that everything in the room had stopped, like the watch and the clock, a long time ago." Dickens' novels were among Dodgson's favorites, and *Great Expectations* appeared serially from 1860 to 1861, just a year before Dodgson told his first extemporaneous Alice stories.

8. The first stanzas of Taylor's poem read,

> Twinkle, twinkle, little star,
> How I wonder what you are!
> Up above the world so high,
> Like a diamond in the sky.

> When the blazing sun is gone,
> When he nothing shines upon,
> Then you show your little light,
> Twinkle, twinkle, all the night.

> Then the traveller in the dark
> Thanks you for your tiny spark:
> He could not see which way to go,
> If you did not twinkle so.
> (1806)

Alice herself is in many ways a "traveller in the dark" world of Wonderland. Like the innocent singer of Taylor's childish verses, she has wondered idly

156

about the nature of the little star "up above" whose distant, precious "little light," although it was growing dimmer, still could be counted on to give her a stable, reliable reference point to guide her in her chaotic underground journey. Without its "tiny spark," without such an immortal diamond in the sky, she senses, she "could not see which way to go." The fearful power of Carroll's subversive parody depends to a great extent on its effective satiric destruction of the sense of security Taylor's familiar sentimental verses provided for so many of her original little readers and listeners. Read in this light, Alice's politely reserved, vaguely cynical comment on the Mad Hatter's hopelessly mixed-up, insane version—"I've heard something like it" (*W*, 57)—sounds a particularly ominous note, suggesting that Alice is here losing touch with her once familiar, reliable guideposts from "up above," as well as her precious sense of wonder and her earlier impulse to correct the by now obviously incorrigible creatures of Wonderland.

9. It should be noted that the Mock Turtle's song that accompanies the Lobster Quadrille reverses Alice's uncontrollable Wonderland practice, twisting the sadistic original—" 'Will you walk into my parlour?' said the spider to the fly"—into an innocuous nursery rhyme. This parody demonstrates in one more way that Wonderland refuses to be consistent to itself: if the aboveground rhymes tend to hide or deny nature's amorality and Darwinian theory, Wonderland's poems will be vengefully Darwinian; but if above-ground rhymes admit the amoral cruelty of nature, then Wonderland produces harmless, sentimental nonsense verses where the creatures of the sea join in a friendly dance or where owls and panthers peacefully share pies.

5. Alice Becomes an *I*

1. Many Carroll critics have interpreted the *Alice* books as myths of growing up. For a good recent example, see Terry Otten, "After Innocence: Alice in the Garden," in *Lewis Carroll: A Celebration,* ed. Edward Guiliano (New York: Clarkson N. Potter, 1982), 55ff. Horace Gregory, in his foreword to the Signet edition of the *Alice* books (New York: 1960), states the case succinctly: "No psychologist has presented a case history of a child's growing up with more firmness, wit, and subtlety than Dodgson" (vii).

It should be noted, however, that Carroll's prefatory poem to *Through the Looking-Glass* seems to deny to Alice any passage from innocence to experience between the two sets of adventures: it begins by addressing her as "child of the pure unclouded brow" and later claims that he and she are "but older children." But just as he turned the cloudy July afternoon in 1862 when he told some of his first extemporaneous *Alice* stories into a "golden," sunny one (see Derek Hudson, *Lewis Carroll: An Illustrated Biography* [New York: Clarkson N. Potter, 1977], 114), just as he slyly allowed Alice only a half year's Carrollian growth for some six or seven years of real growth, in this prefatory poem he seems to sentimentalize the child heroine of *Looking-Glass* whose face "he has not seen" for some time, admitting in the closing poem that the Alice he imagined in the opening poem is an "Alice moving under skies / Never seen by waking eyes."

2. Dodgson's diary entry for 11 February 1856 explains the basic principles of the reversal, formed upon Latinate middle terms: "Lutwidge = Ludovic = Louis [Lewis], and Charles [Carolus]." *The Diaries of Lewis Carroll*, ed. Roger Lancelyn Green (New York: Oxford University Press, 1954), 1:77. But, as one might expect from this author who reveled in complex and arcane word play, the underlying dynamics are more complicated. For one thing, there is a decided shift here from an unambiguous masculinity to a surreptitious femininity—Lutwidge was Dodgson's mother's maiden name and Carroll is often a feminine name; while any reference to the decidedly masculine, patronymic surname Dodgson is eliminated altogether. Moreover, despite Roger Green's (convincing) speculation in the *Diaries* (1:83) that Dodgson probably did not meet Alice Liddell until 25 April 1856, it is very tempting to interpret "Lewis Carroll" (L. C.) as a play on Alice's nickname "Lacie," as well as a play on the double *d*s and double *l*s in Liddell. The notion that Alice is really the stand-in, the dream censor's substitution for the actual dreamer Dodgson, has many adherents among Carroll's psychoanalytic interpreters.

3. Kathleen Blake, *Play, Games, and Sport: The Literary Works of Lewis Carroll* (Ithaca, N. Y., and London: Cornell University Press, 1974), 147.

4. Ibid., 71. Compare Blake on pp. 60–61: "It has been often enough remarked that Carroll (or Dodgson) lived his life, so to speak, according to Hoyle. Florence Becker Lennon says in *Victoria through the Looking-Glass, The Life of Lewis Carroll* (New York: Simon & Schuster, 1945): 'His life was a game, even his logic, his mathematics, and his singular ordering of his household and other affairs. His logic was a game and his games were logical.' . . . Rev. W. Tuckwell, who knew Carroll, states that his 'life [was] mapped out in squares like Alice's landscape.' "

5. The word *manage* is used at several crucial junctures in *Through the Looking-Glass*. See, for example, chapter 9, "Queen Alice," which begins with Alice saying to herself, "If I really am a Queen . . . I shall be able to manage it quite well in time" (*L*, 192). Alice's locution "in time" is noteworthy here, for it is only in the construct of time that managers can manage, only in the construct of time that Alice can mature to queenhood.

6. It should be noted that the furious, mad Queen of Hearts of *Wonderland* is transformed into the much more manageable Red Queen of *Looking-Glass*. This transformation, this lessening of the "red" fury is another indirect marking of Alice's maturation from one book to the sequel. In 1887 Carroll himself noted the distinction: "I pictured to myself the Queen of Hearts as a sort of embodiment of ungovernable passion—a blind and aim-

less Fury. The Red Queen I pictured as a Fury, but of another type; *her* passion must be cold and calm; she must be formal and strict, yet not unkindly; pedantic to the tenth degree, the concentrated essence of all governesses!" (from "*Alice* on the Stage," *The Theatre,* [April 1887]; reprinted in Donald Gray, ed., *Alice in Wonderland: Authoritative Texts of Alice's Adventures in Wonderland, Through the Looking-Glass, The Hunting of the Snark* [New York: Norton, 1971], 281). The emphasis on governance here— "ungovernable," "governesses," "formal and strict"—represents but another mirror reflection of Alice's efficient movement toward self-command by means of a "cold and calm" progression on a formal, arbitrary, and strictly arranged field of play.

7. Nina Auerbach, in "Alice and Wonderland: A Curious Child," *Victorian Studies,* 17 (September 1973): 31–47, consistently makes the point that the creatures of *Wonderland* represent aspects of Alice's own personality. It might be instructive to compare Auerbach's view here with Sandra Gilbert and Susan Gubar's remarks about images of women in the Snow White legend: "To be caught and trapped in a mirror . . . is to be driven inward, obsessively studying self-images as if seeking a viable self." *The Madwoman in the Attic: The Woman Writer and the Nineteenth-Century Imagination* (New Haven: Yale University Press, 1979), 37.

8. Martin Gardner's extensive note (*The Annotated Alice,* 170, 172) on the *Looking-Glass* chess motif includes this remark: "By a happy accident chess also ties in beautifully with the mirror-reflection motif. Not only do rooks, bishops, and knights come in pairs, but the asymmetric arrangement of one player's pieces at the start of a game (asymmetric because of the positions of king and queen) is an exact mirror reflection of his opponent's pieces." It is curious that Gardner attributes the choice of chess to a "happy accident," for it is difficult to think of a more deliberate, less accidental choice by Dodgson, that most deliberate of writers and games players.

9. Alice's power is revealed obliquely in her first moments behind the looking-glass. Tenniel's picture of the frightened and protesting White King in Alice's large and strong hand is matched by the narrator's remark soon after that gentle "Alice was too strong for him" (*L,* 115). In the next chapter, "The Garden of Live Flowers," Alice merely "whispers" to the shouting daisies, "If you don't hold your tongues, I'll pick you!" "There was silence in a moment, and several of the pink daisies turned white" (*L,* 122). Such quiet power, the power of social class in the Oxford world of the 1860s, was a force that Dodgson and the dean's daughter Alice Liddell knew well; here it prefigures Alice's easy accession to queenhood at the conclusion of her adventures.

10. It is worth noting that the treatments of nursery rhymes in the two *Alice* books are almost diametrically opposed: in *Wonderland,* Alice never gets the words of the nursery rhymes right; in *Looking-Glass* the nursery rhymes

and their enactments by the creatures are the same as their originals, thus underscoring the contrast between the license and disorder of Alice's infantile adventures and the regularity and order of her final adventures.

11. In "*Alice* on the Stage" (see note 6), Carroll wrote, "The White Queen seemed, to my dreaming fancy, gentle, stupid, fat and pale; helpless as an *infant*" (Gray 283; my italics).

12. In *Sylvie and Bruno* (1889–93), his final work of fantastic fiction, Carroll makes a macabre joke of the fact that "evil" is merely "live" backwards. Apparently, Dodgson was aware of the possibilities for evil in his overweening desires to live "backwards" in his relations with scores of little-girl friends, his many childish pursuits, his fascination with all things reversed or reversible. In an 1876 letter to Gertrude Chataway, one of his dearest child friends (then 10 years old), Dodgson writes; "When the real warm weather begins again . . . you must beg hard to be brought over to Oxford again. I want to do some better photographs of you: those were not really good ones I did—it was such a wretched day for it. And mind you don't grow a bit older, for I shall want to take you in the same dress again: if anything, you'd better grow a *little* younger—go back to your last birthday but one" (*Letters*, 1:238).

13. "Alice's Invasion of Wonderland," *PMLA* 88, no. 1 (January 1973): 92–93.

6. The *Alices* and the Modern Quest for Order

1. (1929; rpt., New York: Harcourt, Brace & World, 1956), 12–13.

2. Beginning with William Empson's groundbreaking interpretation of the *Alices* in 1935, many critics have read Alice's fall down the rabbit hole and her early adventures in Wonderland as fantasies of reentry into the womb. This reading could be extended to Alice's passage through the looking-glass, another regressive attempt to return to the place from which we emerge, "trailing clouds of glory," as Wordsworth, one of Dodgson's favorite poets and favorite sources for parody, puts it in his ode, "Intimations of Immortality from Recollections of Early Childhood" (1807).

3. Tennyson, like Dodgson, kept up with modern geological and biological science and thus was aware long before the 1859 publication of *The Origin of Species* that the age-old, biblical views of man and his origins were no longer scientifically tenable. Works like Lyell's *The Principles of Geology* (1830–33) and *The Elements of Geology* (1838) and Chambers's *Vestiges of Creation* (1844) had already signaled the direction Darwin would take in his monumental *Origin,* more the capstone of Victorian evolutionary theory than its precipitating event. Thus, passages like the one containing "Nature, red in tooth and claw" were composed, like the *Alices*, in full recognition of the disturbing new views of nature and the place of Homo sapiens in it. See

Notes and References

Christopher Ricks's note on Tennyson's section 56 in *Tennyson: A Selected Edition*, 398.

4. "The Darkling Thrush," lines 25–32, in *The Complete Poetical Works of Thomas Hardy*, vol. 1, ed. Samuel Hynes (Oxford: Clarendon Press, 1982), 188.

5. "The Idea of Order at Key West" (1935), lines 48 and 51–54, in *The Collected Poems of Wallace Stevens* (New York: Knopf, 1964), 130.

6. "Anecdote of the Jar" (1923), line 9, in *Collected Poems of Wallace Stevens*, 76.

7. *Heart of Darkness: An Authoritative Text, Backgrounds and Sources, Essays in Criticism*, ed. Robert Kimbrough (New York: Norton, 1963), 77, 79.

8. This notion of the artist as suspect games player, as artificer and forger of self and cosmos that I have associated with Carroll and his Alice is probably most familiar in connection with the principal figure in modernist English fiction, James Joyce. And in fact Joyce was tremendously indebted to Carroll: his *Finnegans Wake* (1922–39) depends heavily on Carrollian portmanteau words and abounds in witty allusions to Carroll and Carroll's fantasies. See, for example, Anne McGarrity Buki's "Lewis Carroll in Finnegans Wake" in *Lewis Carroll: A Celebration*, ed. Edward Guiliano, 154–66. See also James Atherton's *The Books at the Wake: A Study of Literary Allusions in James Joyce's "Finnegans Wake"* (New York: Viking, 1960), passim. Atherton demonstrates that "many of the wildest and most startling features of *Finnegans Wake* are merely the logical development, or working out on a larger scale, of ideas that first occurred to Lewis Carroll" (124). Many other scholars have noted that Joyce's major works are permeated with Lewis Carroll allusions. When Joyce alludes in *Finnegans Wake* to Dodgson as "Dodgfather, Dogson and Coo," his joke is especially significant for those interested in the role of the modern artist. Now the literary artist, through his playing with words, his naming of things, and particularly with his ability to create new words, actually creates as God creates. Moreover, he creates himself, even if what he creates is a cosmic joke. The fact that Joyce's new comic trinity represents three aspects of Dodgson/Carroll as jokester-artist, the fact that for the Holy Spirit he substitutes the "coo" of a dove (the traditional figure of the Holy Spirit) is more than a good joke. It recognizes that this third figure is more than the sum of the first two, is something beyond the personality of the creator. The new holy spirit or dove is at once a silly "coo," a crass commerical allusion ("co." for "company"), and the inspiring muse, the unexpected inspiration of modern comic geniuses like Carroll and Joyce.

9. Florence Becker Lennon, *The Life of Lewis Carroll* (New York: Collier, 1962), 10. First published as *Victoria through the Looking-Glass: The Life of Lewis Carroll*.

7. What's So Funny about the *Alices*?

1. "Wonderland Revisited," *Kenyon Review* 27 (1956); reprinted in *Aspects of Alice*, ed. Robert Phillips (New York: Vanguard Press, 1971), 189. In the year of Dodgson's death, his nephew Stuart Dodgson Collingwood published the first full-length study of Carroll. *The Life and Letters of Lewis Carroll (Rev. C. L. Dodgson)*, in which Collingwood says of *Wonderland*, "The whole idea came like an inspiration into [Carroll's] mind, and that sort of inspiration does not often come more than once in a lifetime. Nothing which he wrote afterwards had anything like the same amount of freshness, of wit, of real genius. The 'Looking-Glass' most closely approached it in these qualities, but then it was only the following out of the same idea" (106).

2. Empson, "Alice in Wonderland: The Child as Swain," in *Some Versions of Pastoral*, 253–94; Harry Morgan Ayres, *Carroll's Alice* (New York: Columbia University Press, 1936).

3. Martin Gardner, ed., *The Annotated Alice* (1960) and *More Annotated Alice* (1990); Peter Heath, ed., *The Philosopher's Alice* (London: Academy Editors, 1974); James Kincaid, ed., *Alice's Adventures in Wonderland* (Berkeley: University of California Press, 1982) and *Through the Looking-Glass and What Alice Found There* (Berkeley: University of California Press, 1983).

4. See Donald Rackin, "Corrective Laughter: Carroll's Alice and Popular Children's Literature of the Nineteenth Century," *Journal of Popular Culture* 1 (1967): 243–55. See also *The Annotated Alice* and *More Annotated Alice*, ed. Gardner.

5. See, for example, Peter Alexander, "Logic and the Humour of Lewis Carroll," *Proceedings of the Leeds Philosophical and Literary Society* 6 (1951): 551–66; George Pitcher, "Wittgenstein, Nonsense and Lewis Carroll," *Massachusetts Review* 6 (Spring-Summer 1965): 591–611; Taylor, *The White Knight: A Study of C. L. Dodgson;* and Heath, *The Philosopher's Alice.*

6. Katherine Anne Porter, Bertrand Russell, and Mark Van Doren, "Lewis Carroll: *Alice in Wonderland*," a radio panel discussion, in *New Invitation to Learning*, ed. Mark Van Doren (New York: New Home Library, 1942), 208.

7. Quoted by Stanley Edgar Hyman in *The Armed Vision* (New York: Vintage, 1955), 264.

8. Paul Schilder, "Psychoanalytic Remarks on *Alice in Wonderland* and Lewis Carroll," *Journal of Nervous and Mental Diseases* 87 (1938): 159–68.

9. See Sigmund Freud, *Jokes and Their Relations to the Unconscious*, trans. and ed. James Strachey (New York: Norton, 1960); and Freud, "Humour," in *Collected Papers*, vol. 5, trans. Joan Riviere, ed. James Strachey (London: Hogarth Press, 1956).

10. Compare Freud, "Humour," 216–18:

Like wit and the comic, humour has in it a liberating element. But it also has something fine and elevating, which is lacking in the other two ways of deriving pleasure from intellectual activity. Obviously, what is fine about it is the triumph of narcissism, the ego's victorious assertion of its own invulnerability. It refuses to be hurt by the arrows of reality or to be compelled to suffer. It insists that it is impervious to wounds dealt by the outside world. The denial of the claim of reality and the triumph of the pleasure principle cause humour to approximate to regressive or reactionary processes which engage our attention so largely in psychopathology. By its repudiation of the possibility of suffering, it takes its place in the great series of methods devised by the mind of man for evading the compulsion to suffer. Now in what does this humorous attitude consist, by means of which one refuses to undergo suffering, asseverates the invincibility of one's ego against the real world and victoriously upholds the pleasure principle, yet all without quitting the ground of mental sanity, as happens when other means to the same end are adopted? . . . If we turn to consider the situation in which one person adopts a humorous attitude towards others, one view which I have already tentatively suggested in my book on wit will seem very evident. It is this: that the one is adopting towards the other the attitude of an adult towards a child, recognizing and smiling at the triviality of the interests and sufferings which seem to the child so big. Thus the humorist acquires his superiority by assuming the role of the grown-up identifying himself to some extent with the father, while he reduces the other people to the position of children.

11. Virginia Woolf, "Lewis Carroll," in *The Moment and Other Essays* (New York: Harcourt, Brace & World, 1948), 81–83.

12. *"Alice* on the Stage," quoted in Gray, ed., 281–83.

13. An extended psychoanalytic interpretation of the similarities between Swift and Carroll can be found in Phyllis Greenacre's *Swift and Carroll: A Psychoanalytic Study of Two Lives* (New York: International Universities Press, 1955).

14. See, for example, Max Brod, *Franz Kafka: A Biography,* 2d ed., trans. G. Humphreys Roberts and Richard Winston (New York: Schocken, 1960).

15. Among the many *Alice* editions illustrated by artists other than Tenniel, several offer illustrations that reflect the macabre terror in Carroll's drawings. See, for example, the 1969 Random House edition illustrated by the great surrealist painter Salvador Dali and the 1982–83 University of California Press editions illustrated with Barry Moser's excellent woodcuts.

8. Death, Love, and the White Knight's Farewell

1. In her provocative biography, Anne Clark stresses love as a formative element in Dodgson's character and makes a rather convincing case that Dodgson wanted to marry Alice Liddell. See Clark's *Lewis Carroll: A Biography* (New York: Schocken, 1979).

2. "*Alice* on the Stage," quoted in Gray, 283.

3. "*Alice* on the Stage," quoted in Gray, 283. This highly sentimentalized view of Alice's nature is not of course always sustained by the evidence in the *Alice* texts. Several shrewd critics have in their analyses made a point of Alice's flaws and shortcomings. See, for example, Kincaid, "Alice's Invasion of Wonderland"; Nina Auerbach, "Alice in Wonderland: A Curious Child," *Victorian Studies;* and Heath's Introduction to *The Philosopher's Alice.* Carroll himself joked, just two years after the publication of *Wonderland,* that his book about Alice was, he thought, about "malice"—*A Selection from the Letters of Lewis Carroll to his Child-Friends,* ed. Evelyn Hatch (London: Macmillan, 1933), 48.

4. Elizabeth Sewell, *The Field of Nonsense* (London: Chatto & Windus, 1952); hereafter cited in the text as Sewell.

5. Several Carroll critics, on the other hand, have pointed out that the *Alice*s are not, technically, nonsense at all. In his introduction to *The Philosopher's Alice,* Peter Heath makes the point forcefully: "Carroll's fame as a nonsense-writer is by now so firmly established that it is probably too late to persuade anyone that, apart from a few isolated instances such as the *Jabberwock* poem, he is not strictly a writer of nonsense at all. . . . Carroll stands at the opposite pole from the true nonsense-writer. Although as a literary category the term had not been invented in his day, the proper genre is that of the absurd."

6. In *The Complete Works of Lewis Carroll,* introduction by Alexander Woollcott (London: Modern Library, 1937), 1079–88; hereafter cited in the text as "Novelty and Romancement."

7. Although Alice Liddell was ten years old when Dodgson probably told first his extemporaneous Alice tale (1862), she is seven in *Wonderland* (1865) and only seven and a half in *Looking-Glass* (1872). The heartfelt Carrollian arithmetic here occurs in a number of places, such as the celebration of un-birthdays—that is, the celebration of *not* growing older.

8. This passage has of course a distinct sexual connotation. Although sex has a relatively small independent role in the *Alice*s, here sex is used to underscore the frightening transience of life, conflating into a kind of macabre "portmanteau" bed the first flush of full human development with its last gasp.

9. From the recently discovered Carroll manuscript, *The Wasp in a Wig: A "Suppressed" Episode of Through the Looking-Glass and What Alice*

Found There, with a preface, introduction, and notes by Martin Gardner (New York: The Lewis Carroll Society of North America, 1977), 19; hereafter cited in the text as *Wasp.* Although some scholars consider this episode an unnecessary repetition of the White Knight scene, Carroll obviously did not. He saw it through the galley-proof stage and carefully corrected the galleys. A probable explanation for the "suppression" is that Tenniel saw himself caricatured in the Wasp and chose not to join his collaborator Carroll in his self-mocking but loving farewell to their mutual invention Alice. Tenniel (1820–1914), by the way, was some twelve years older than Dodgson.

10. Victorian fiction offers a host of parallel instances of this regenerative power the loving young can spark in the dying old. Among them the most widely known, perhaps, are the deathbed reconciliations of Miss Havisham and Mrs. Joe Gargery with Pip in Dickens's *Great Expectations* (1861).

11. "Alice on the Stage," quoted in Gray, 281–82 (Carroll's italics).

12. See particularly Wordsworth's great ode, "Intimations of Immortality from Recollections of Early Childhood" (1807), arguably the single-most influential English poem of the entire nineteenth century.

13. William Wordsworth, "Intimations of Immortality," lines 164–69.

14. Gardner, ed., *The Annotated Alice,* 311.

15. Gardner's note on page 44 of *The Annotated Alice* represents the scholarly consensus on this matter: "The Duck is Reverend Duckworth; the Lory (an Australian parrot) is Lorina Liddell; Edith Liddell is the Eaglet; and the Dodo is Lewis Carroll himself. When Carroll stammered he pronounced his name 'Do-Do-Dodgson'.... When the facsimile edition of the [*under Ground*] manuscript was published in 1886, Duckworth received a copy inscribed, 'The Duck from the Dodo.'"

Selected Bibliography

Primary Works

Critical Editions

Alice in Wonderland: Authoritative Texts of Alice's Adventures in Wonderland, Through the Looking-Glass, The Hunting of the Snark; Backgrounds and Essays in Criticism. Edited by Donald J. Gray. New York: W. W. Norton, 1971. A revised, second edition of this collection is scheduled for publication in 1992.

Alice's Adventures in Wonderland: A Critical Handbook. Edited by Donald Rackin. Belmont, Calif.: Wadsworth, 1969. Includes a facsimile of the *Alice's Adventures under Ground* manuscript and 12 critical essays.

Alice's Adventures in Wonderland and *Through the Looking-Glass and What Alice Found There,* 2 vols. Illustrated by Barry Moser. Preface and notes by James R. Kincaid. Berkeley: University of California Press, 1982, 1983.

The Annotated Alice: Alice's Adventures in Wonderland and Through the Looking-Glass. Introduction and edited by Martin Gardner. New York: Clarkson N. Potter, 1960. Extensive, detailed notes.

The Annotated Snark. Introduction and notes by Martin Gardner. New York: Bramhall House, 1962.

The Complete Illustrated Works of Lewis Carroll. Edited by Edward Guiliano. New York: Avenel, 1982.

The Complete Works of Lewis Carroll. Introduction by Alexander Woollcott. New York: Modern Library, n. d. (1937).

More Annotated Alice. Notes by Martin Gardner. New York: Random House, 1990. A sequel to *The Annotated Alice* (1960), with a new set of extensive notes, illustrated by Peter Newell.

The Wasp in a Wig: A "Suppressed" Episode of Through the Looking-Glass and What Alice Found There. Preface, introduction, and notes by Martin Gardner. New York: Lewis Carroll Society of North America, 1977.

Correspondence and Diaries

The Diaries of Lewis Carroll. Edited by Roger Lancelyn Green. 2 vols. New York: Oxford University Press, 1953.

The Letters of Lewis Carroll. Edited by Morton N. Cohen. 2 vols. New York: Oxford University Press, 1979.

Lewis Carroll and the House of Macmillan. Edited by Morton N. Cohen and Anita Gandolfo. Cambridge: Cambridge University Press, 1987. A collection of correspondence between Carroll and his publishers.

Secondary Works

Bibliographies

Fordyce, Rachel. *Lewis Carroll: A Reference Guide.* Boston: G. K. Hall, 1988. The best source for comprehensive coverage and detailed annotations of all secondary materials since the late 1950s.

Guiliano, Edward. *Lewis Carroll: An Annotated International Bibliography, 1960–77.* Charlottesville: University Press of Virginia, 1980.

———. "Lewis Carroll: A Sesquicentennial Guide to Research." *Dickens Studies Annual: Essays on Victorian Fiction* 10 (1982): 263–310. A useful narrative account of major trends in Carroll scholarship.

Williams, Sidney Herbert, and Falconer Madan. The Lewis Carroll Handbook. 1931. Revised and augmented by Roger Lancelyn Green. London: Oxford University Press, 1962. Further revised by Dennis Crutch. Folkstone, England, and Hamden, Conn.: Dawson/Archon Books, 1979.

Essay Collections

Bloom, Harold, ed. *Modern Critical Views: Lewis Carroll.* New York: Chelsea House, 1987. Twelve recently published pieces of Carroll criticism, marred by the omission of the original footnotes.

Gray, Donald J., ed. *Alice in Wonderland,* Norton Critical Edition, 1971. Contains nine critical essays.

Guiliano, Edward, ed. *Lewis Carroll: A Celebration. Essays on the Occasion of the 150th Anniversary of the Birth of Charles Lutwidge Dodgson.*

New York: Clarkson N. Potter, 1982. Fifteen essays, some by recognized Carroll experts, on a wide range of Carroll texts and issues.

————, ed. *Lewis Carroll Observed: A Collection of Unpublished Photographs, Drawings, Poetry, and New Essays.* New York: Potter/Crown, 1976. Fourteen essays, many by leading Carroll scholars.

Guiliano, Edward, and Kincaid, James R., eds. *Soaring with the Dodo: Essays on Lewis Carroll's Life and Art.* Charlottesville: University of Virginia Press, 1982. A bound volume of the *English Language Notes* special Lewis Carroll issue (20, no. 2 [December 1982]) containing ten critical essays by leading Carroll scholars.

Phillips, Robert, ed. *Aspects of Alice: Lewis Carroll's Dreamchild as Seen through the Critics' Looking-Glasses 1865–1971.* New York: Vanguard Press, 1971. Thirty-nine essays: the largest, most comprehensive collection of critical essays on the *Alices.*

Rackin, Donald, ed. *Alice's Adventures in Wonderland: A Critical Handbook.* Belmont, Calif.: Wadsworth, 1969. Contains 12 critical essays.

Critical Studies: Books

Ayres, Harry Morgan. *Carroll's Alice.* New York: Columbia University Press, 1936. One of the first serious academic treatments of the *Alices,* it includes a detailed comparison of the first (withdrawn) and second editions of *Wonderland.* Portion reprinted in Rackin.

Blake, Kathleen. *Play, Games, and Sport: The Literary Works of Lewis Carroll.* Ithaca, N. Y., and London: Cornell University Press, 1974. Traces in Carroll's major works the "shapes . . . cast by a playful aesthetic idea and a world view that sees games all around." Includes an informative chapter on Victorian attitudes toward amusements.

Clark, Anne. *Lewis Carroll: A Biography.* New York: Shocken, 1979. The best, most comprehensive recent critical biography. Especially useful for its detailed account of Dodgson's early years and the influence of religion.

————. *The Real Alice: Lewis Carroll's Dream Child.* London: Michael Joseph, 1981. First full biography of Alice Pleasance Liddell, the model for Carroll's Alice.

Collingwood, Stuart Dodgson. *The Life and Letters of Lewis Carroll (Rev. C. L. Dodgson).* New York: Century Co., 1899. The authorized biography by Dodgson's nephew, published in England in 1898, the year of Dodgson's death.

De la Mare, Walter. *Lewis Carroll.* London: Faber & Faber, 1932. A famous poet's impressionistic critical study concentrating on the *Alice* books. Portions reprinted in Phillips, Rackin.

Gernsheim, Helmut. *Lewis Carroll, Photographer.* 1949. Rev. ed. New York:

Dover Publications, 1969. The best critical book on Carroll's photographic achievement; includes many of his finest photographs.

Greenacre, Phyllis. *Swift and Carroll: A Psychoanalytic Study of Two Lives.* New York: International Universities Press, 1955. An eminent psychoanalyst applies her Freudian theory to Carroll and his works. Portions reprinted in Gray, Phillips, Rackin.

Hancher, Michael. *The Tenniel Illustrations to the "Alice" Books.* Columbus: Ohio University Press, 1985. A richly illustrated study of Tenniel's work and the nature of the Carroll-Tenniel collaboration.

Heath, Peter. *The Philosopher's Alice.* London: Academy Editors, 1974. An annotated edition: notes from a professional philosopher's perspective. Introduction reprinted in Bloom.

Hudson, Derek. *Lewis Carroll: An Illustrated Biography.* New York: Clarkson N. Potter, 1977. A dependable biography that generally avoids literary analysis. Portions reprinted in Gray, Rackin.

Huxley, Francis. *The Raven and the Writing Desk.* London: Thames & Hudson, 1976. Concentrates on logic and wordplay in Carroll.

Kelly, Richard. *Lewis Carroll.* 1977. Rev. ed. Boston: Twayne, 1990. A critical biography, including detailed analyses of the *Alices*.

Kirk, Daniel F. *Charles Dodgson, Semiotician.* Humanities Monograph Series, no. 11. Gainesville, Fla.: University of Florida Press, 1963. An approach to Carroll as a forerunner of modern linguistic theory.

Lennon, Florence Becker. *Victoria through the Looking-Glass: The Life of Lewis Carroll.* New York: Dover, 1972; London: Constable, 1972. A second revision of *Victoria through the Looking-Glass,* 1945, and *The Life of Lewis Carroll,* 1962. One of the best critical biographies of Carroll; inventive and insightful. Portion reprinted in Phillips.

Ovenden, Graham, ed. *The Illustrators of Alice in Wonderland and Through the Looking-Glass.* 1973. Rev. ed. London: Academy, 1979. A selection from the works of more than 100 illustrators, most from the twentieth century.

Reed, Langford. *The Life of Lewis Carroll.* London: W. & G. Foyle, Ltd., 1932. Stresses the split-personality view.

Sewell, Elizabeth. *The Field of Nonsense.* London: Chatto & Windus, 1952. A comprehensive study of nonsense and how it works in Carroll and Lear. Portions reprinted in Gray, Rackin.

Sutherland, Robert D. *Language and Lewis Carroll.* The Hague: Mouton, 1970. How Carroll applied his linguistic knowledge in his comic works.

Taylor, Alexander, L. *The White Knight: A Study of C. L. Dodgson (Lewis Carroll).* London: Oliver & Boyd, 1952. Stresses the importance of layers of meaning in the *Alices*—particularly the philosophical, scientific, and mathematical layers. Portion reprinted in Phillips.

Weaver, Warren. *Alice in Many Tongues: The Translations of "Alice in Wonderland."* Madison: University of Wisconsin Press, 1964. A comprehensive survey of translations, including a useful checklist.

Critical Studies: Articles and Parts of Books

Alexander, Peter. "Logic and the Humour of Lewis Carroll." *Proceedings of the Leeds Philosophical and Literary Society* 6 (1951): 551–66. One of the best logical explanations of Carroll's comic effects.

Atherton, James S. "Carroll: The Unforeseen Precursor." In *The Books at the Wake: A Study of Literary Allusions in James Joyce's Finnegans Wake,* 124–36. New York: Viking, 1960. Demonstrates Carroll's major influence on many of the "wildest and most startling features of *Finnegans Wake.*"

Auden, W. H. "Today's 'Wonder-World' Needs Alice." *New York Times Magazine,* 1 July 1962, sec. 6, pp. 5ff. Recounts Auden's own fascination with the *Alices.* Reprinted in Phillips.

Auerbach, Nina. "Alice and Wonderland: A Curious Child." *Victorian Studies* 17 (September 1973): 31–47. Examines various aspects of the child Alice, real and imaginary, including Alice's violent elements as well her passive, "pure" side. Reprinted in Bloom.

———. "Falling Alice, Fallen Women, and Victorian Dream Children." *English Language Notes* 20, no. 2 (December 1982): 46–64. Enumerates various critical interpretations of Alice, compares Dodgson's child photographs with Victorian iconography, and relates these issues to Dodgson's respect for his child friends.

Bivona, Daniel. "Alice the Child-Imperialist and the Games of Wonderland." *Nineteenth-Century Fiction* 41, no. 2 (September 1986): 143–71. Examines Alice's relationships to the imperialism of her day and looks at mastery through mastering the "game" and reconstructing the story.

Blake, Kathleen. "Three Alices, Three Carrolls." *English Language Notes* 20, no. 2 (December 1982): 131–38. A review article based on the essays in Edward Guiliano's *Lewis Carroll: A Celebration;* outlines three primary strains in current Carroll criticism.

Cohen, Morton N. "Lewis Carroll and the House of Macmillan." *Browning Institute Studies* 7 (1979): 31–70. Examines Carroll's long relationship with his publisher, Macmillan.

Culler, A. Dwight. "The Darwinian Revolution and Literary Form." In *The Art of Victorian Prose,* edited by George Levine and William Madden,

224–46. London: Oxford University Press, 1968. Compares the similarities between Carroll's and Darwin's philosophical visions.

Eagleton, Terry. "Alice and Anarchy." *New Blackfriars 53*, no. 629 (October 1972): 447–55. Develops a theory of games and applies it to the *Alices*.

Empson, William. *"Alice in Wonderland:* The Child as Swain." In *Some Versions of the Pastoral,* 253–94. London: Chatto & Windus, 1935. Often cited as one of the most perceptive analyses of Carroll's major fictions; emphasizes the subversive nature of the *Alices*. Reprinted in Gray, Phillips, and Rackin.

Gordon, Jan B. "The *Alice* Books and the Metaphors of Victorian Childhood." In *Aspects of Alice,* edited by Robert Phillips 93–113. Views the *Alices* as decadent adult literature. Reprinted in Bloom.

Gordon, Jan B., and Guiliano, Edward. "From Victorian Textbook to Ready-Made: Lewis Carroll and the Black Art." *English Language Notes* 20 (December 1982): 1–25. On connections between Carroll's photography and his fictions.

Gregory, Horace. Foreword to *Alice's Adventures in Wonderland and Through the Looking-Glass.* Signet Classics. v–x. New York: New American Library, 1960. A brief but perceptive general analysis of the *Alices*.

Guiliano, Edward. "A Time for Humor: Lewis Carroll, Laughter and Despair, and *The Hunting of the Snark.*" In *Lewis Carroll: A Celebration,* edited by Edward Guiliano, 123–31. Demonstrates important relationships between *The Hunting of the Snark* and the *Alices*. Reprinted in Bloom.

Hardy, Barbara. "Fantasy and Dream." In *Tellers and Listeners: The Narrative Imagination,* 33–45. London: Athlone, 1975. Carroll's Alice compared to other daydreamers in literature–especially Kafka's K.

Henkle, Roger. "Carroll's Narratives Underground: 'Modernism' and Form." In *Lewis Carroll: A Celebration,* edited by Edward Guiliano, 89–100. Generic aspects of the *Alices* that make them "modern."

Holquist, Michael. "What Is a Boojum? Nonsense and Modernism." *Yale French Studies* 43 (1969): 145–64. *The Hunting of the Snark* as a major precursor of literary modernism, especially in its self-sufficient structure. Reprinted in Gray.

Kenner, Hugh. "Alice in Chapelizoid." In *Dublin's Joyce,* 276–300. London: Chatto & Windus, 1955. Discusses important similarities between Carroll and Joyce.

Kincaid, James R. "Alice's Invasion of Wonderland." *PMLA* 88, no. 1 (January 1973): 92–99. Reads Alice's rejections of the worlds underground and behind the mirror as, in part, rejections of comic liberation.

Leach, Elsie. *"Alice in Wonderland* in Perspective." *Victorian Newsletter* no. 25 (Spring 1964): 9–11. Views the *Alices* as a strong reaction against the didacticism of earlier children's literature. Reprinted in Phillips.

Levin, Harry. "Wonderland Revisited." *Kenyon Review* 27, no. 4 (1965): 591–616. Explores Carroll's motivations for writing *Wonderland*. Reprinted in Phillips.

Lurie, Alison. *Don't Tell the Grown-Ups: Subversive Children's Literature.* Boston: Little, Brown & Co., 1990. Some perceptive remarks on *Alices*.

Madden, William A. "Framing the *Alices.*" *PMLA* 101 (1986): 362–73. Assesses the functions of the *Alice* frame stories.

Morton, Lionel. "Memory in the *Alice* Books." *Nineteenth-Century Fiction* 33 (1978): 285–308. Nostalgia in the *Alices* and Wordsworth.

Otten, Terry. "After Innocence: Alice in the Garden." In *Lewis Carroll: A Celebration,* edited by Edward Guiliano, 50–61. Analyzes the changes in Alice's perception from *Wonderland* to *Looking-Glass.*

Pitcher, George. "Wittgenstein, Nonsense, and Lewis Carroll." *Massachusetts Review* 6 (Spring–Summer 1965): 591–611. Discovers various similarities between the two logicians, especially regarding nonsense. Reprinted in Gray.

Polhemus, Robert M. "Carroll's *Through the Looking-Glass* (1871): The Comedy of Regression." In *Comic Faith: The Great Tradition from Austen to Joyce,* 245–93. Chicago: University of Chicago Press, 1980. Stresses the regressive escapism in Carroll's comedy.

Rackin, Donald. "Alice's Journey to the End of Night." *PMLA* 81, no. 5 (October 1966): 313–26. A close reading of *Wonderland* as existential myth. Reprinted in Phillips, Rackin.

———. "Blessed Rage: Lewis Carroll and the Modern Rage for Order." In *Lewis Carroll: A Celebration,* edited by Edward Guiliano, 15–25. Dodgson's obsessive rage for order shapes the themes and literary strategies of the *Alices.*

———. "Laughing and Grief: What's So Funny about *Alice In Wonderland?*" In *Lewis Carroll Observed,* edited by Edward Guiliano, 1–18. Analyzes the polar dynamics of Carroll's comedy.

———. "Love and Death in Carroll's *Alices.*" *English Language Notes* 20 (December 1982): 26–54. Dodgson's love of Alice emerges from his strong sense of mortality. Reprinted in Bloom.

Schilder, Paul. "Psychoanalytic Remarks on *Alice in Wonderland* and Lewis Carroll." *Journal of Nervous and Mental Diseases* 87 (1938): 159–68. Frequently cited early essay by a professional psychiatrist who warns against children reading the *Alices* because they are too regressive. Reprinted in Phillips.

Sewell, Elizabeth. "The Nonsense System in Lewis Carroll's Work and in Today's World." In *Lewis Carroll Observed,* edited by Edward Guiliano, 60–67. Updates and revises Sewell's celebrated *The Field of Nonsense,* 1952.

Spacks, Patricia Meyer. "Logic and Nonsense in *Through the Looking-Glass.*" *ETC: A Review of General Semantics* 18, no. 1 (1961): 91–100. Carroll's preoccupation with language in *Looking-Glass.* Reprinted in Phillips.

Stern, Jeffrey. "Lewis Carroll the Surrealist." In *Lewis Carroll Observed,* edited by Edward Guiliano, 132–43. How Carroll relates to the surrealistic movement of the twentieth century.

Van Doren, Mark. "Lewis Carroll: *Alice in Wonderland.*" In *The New Invitation to Learning.* New York: New Home Library, 1942. A radio broadcast of a conversation about the *Alices* by Van Doren, Katherine Anne Porter, and Betrand Russell.

Wilson, Edmund. "C. L. Dodgson: The Poet Logician." In *The Shores of Light,* 540–50. New York: Farrar, Straus & Giroux, 1952. Deplores the lack of serious critical attention to Carroll's fantasies. Reprinted in Phillips, Rackin.

Woolf, Virginia. "Lewis Carroll." In *The Moment and Other Essays,* 81–83. New York: Harcourt, 1948. Reprinted in Woolf's *Collected Essays.* New York: Harcourt, Brace & World, 1967. Suggests that Dodgson holds childhood crystallized in himself and in his *Alices.* Reprinted in Phillips, Rackin.

Index

Index

Eliot, George, 10, 12, 150
Empson, William, 23, 107, 108, 154n4, 156n4, 160n2
Engels, Friedrich, 8
Erikson, Erik, 23

Fordyce, Rachel, 23, 29, 154n7
Freud, Anna, 23
Freud, Sigmund: and Freudianism, 10, 17, 22–23, 68, 108, 113, 124, 162n10. *See also* Comedy in the *Alice* books, Freudian aspects

Gardner, Martin, 26, 107, 144, 155n2, 159n8, 165n15
Gilbert, William Schwenck, and Sullivan, Arthur Seymour, 9, 12
Green, Roger Lancelyn, 18, 25, 30
Greenacre, Phyllis, 23
Guiliano, Edward, 26–27, 29, 154n7

Hardy, Thomas, 97–98
Hargreaves, Alice P. Liddell. *See* Liddell, Alice Pleasance
Heath, Peter, 28, 107, 164n3, 164n5
Hume, Kathryn, 19
Hudson, Derek, 25

Jung, Carl, 23, 68
Joyce, James, 161n8

Kafka, Franz, 19, 110, 116, 124, 156n5
Kincaid, James R., 26, 86, 107, 164n3
Krutch, Joseph Wood, 88

Lacan, Jacques, 23
Lear, Edward, 12, 130
Lennon, Florence Becker, 23, 103, 158n4
Levin, Harry, 23

Liddell, Alice Pleasance (Mrs. Alice Hargreaves), 25, 31, 35, 69, 73, 84, 87, 90, 102, 115, 128, 130, 136, 142, 143, 144, 151–52, 164n7. *See also* Characters in the *Alice* books, Alice
Liddell, Henry George, 9

Marx, Karl, 8, 9, 23
Meredith, George, 12, 150
Mill, John Stuart, 10
Moore, Thomas, 144–45

Paley, William, 95–96
Pater, Walter, 10
Poe, Edgar Allan, 132, 133
Porter, Katherine Anne, 108

Reed, Langford, 24
Richards, I. A., 108
Rossetti, Christina, 26
Rossetti, Dante Gabriel, 26
Ruskin, John, 6, 10, 26, 146
Russell, Bertrand, 28

Schilder, Paul, 108
Sewell, Elizabeth, 28, 130–31
Shakespeare, William, 13, 96, 116, 127, 137–38
Shaw, George Bernard, 12
Smiles, Samuel, 12
Southey, Robert, 47
Stevens, Wallace, 100, 101–2
Swift, Jonathan, 116, 163n13

Taylor, Alexander L., 155n2
Taylor, Jane, 55–56, 156n8
Tenniel, John, 117, 124–25, 138, 149, 159n9, 164n9
Tennyson, Alfred, Lord, 7, 26, 52, 77–78, 93–94, 97, 160n3
Terry, Ellen, 26
Thackeray, William Makepeace, 12
Trollope, Anthony, 12

177

The Author

Donald Rackin is a professor of English at Temple University in Philadelphia, where he has taught Victorian literature and modern English and American fiction since 1962. He has published widely on Lewis Carroll since his 1966 *PMLA* prize-winning article, "Alice's Journey to the End of Night," and is generally considered one of the world's leading Carroll critics.